Becoming Safely Embodied

ADVANCE PRAISE FOR
Becoming Safely Embodied

This is a wonderfully effective, practical book. With Deirdre Fay's vast clinical experience, it is both grounded in science and soaring with heart and spirit. Steadily, compassionately, and wisely, she guides us in coming home to our deepest selves and the truly safe harbor we find there.

—**Rick Hanson, Ph.D.,** Author of *Neurodharma:*
New Science, Ancient Wisdom, and Seven Practices
of the Highest Happiness

Isn't feeling safely embodied what all trauma survivors long for? Deirdre Fay offers an utterly trustworthy guide for getting there, based on her personal experience of trauma and years of collaboration with top experts in the field. With a focus on enhancing resources rather than uncovering old wounds, Deirdre Fay's thoughtful and compassionate model is a valuable addition to any trauma treatment. Highly recommended!

—**Christopher Germer, Ph.D.,** Faculty, Harvard Medical School and author
of *The Mindful Path to Self-Compassion*

In *Becoming Safely Embodied,* Deirdre Fay invites trauma survivors on a journey to living an embodied life. Her deep understanding of suffering and the healing power of belonging is woven into the pages of this beautifully written skills manual. Drawing on her wisdom from years of working with trauma survivors she brings spirituality and psychology together in a series of simple, yet powerful skills that support survivors in coming home to their bodies. *Becoming Safely Embodied* skillfully engages the pull toward healing that is an inherent part of the human experience. With her clinical expertise and deep compassion, Deirdre Fay is a trusted guide to creating pathways to embodied wellbeing.

—**Deb Dana, LCSW,** Author of *The Polyvagal Theory in Therapy: Engaging*
the Rhythm of Regulation and *Polyvagal Exercises for Safety and Connection: 50*
Client-Centered Practices

This beautiful and wise book will be a boon to anyone wanting to integrate mindfulness, body-awareness, and yoga into helping to manage the physiological and psychological aftermath of trauma. Full of practical guidance and exercises, this re-published book is as vital and relevant as ever, especially its central thread of the importance of safe embodiment as the sine qua non of healing from trauma

—**Graham Music, Ph.D.,** Consultant psychotherapist, Tavistock Centre, London and author of *Nurturing Children, Nurturing Natures,* and *The Good Life*

Welcome to the new, updated and remarkable resource, Becoming Safely Embodied! Many individuals who have experienced early childhood trauma are phobic of their bodies, because the body is the location of their suffering, the home of sensations that underlie painful emotions and memories, the scene of experiences that were intolerable. Yet our bodies are also a powerful source of healing, of regulation and a sense of wellbeing. Deirdre Fay has written an impressive and gentle guide for people to develop a step-wise and careful acquaintance with one's body, to harness the power of physical grounding and regulation and to learn to become more comfortable with and in one's body. The skills and practices of *Becoming Safely Embodied* have been used successfully for many years in inpatient programs and in private practices around the world, both in groups and with individuals. This book is a compassionate, and rich source of practical help that respects the pace of the individual, a truly timeless and invaluable resource for those who have been traumatized and those who strive to help them.

—**Kathy Steele, MN, CS,** Private practice owner, Atlanta GA and author of *Treating Trauma-Related Dissociation: A Practical Integrative Approach*

Deirdre Fay is the consummate guide to cultivating a secure inner relationship with your wise mind and heart. Her work with embodiment, compassion, and personal liberation has liberated the lives of thousands of people, and this book is a personal journey with her to a place of safeness and wholehearted living. Highly recommended.

—**Dennis Tirch, Ph.D.,** Director, The Center for Compassion Focused Therapy

The *Becoming Safely Embodied* principles and practices are a remarkably clear and accessible integration of what we know from the science of trauma and of healing from trauma. Deirdre has humanized the science and brings to this tremendously useful map and guidebook her own deep qualities of warmth and wisdom. If you are someone who is on the path of healing from trauma, or who is dedicated to helping others on that path of healing, or if you are both a sufferer and a healer, this book will be of great benefit. Not only does it help as a guide for healing, but each of the Skills that are integral to Deirdre's program provides for strengthening the core elements of well-being. If we develop these core elements—including a sense of belonging, the capacity to be present in our bodies and in all our dimensions, focusing and directing attention as needed, the ability to recognize and regulate our emotions in healthy ways, the freedom to take a variety of perspectives on ourselves and others—we can both heal and also become more able to flourish as our unique and fully interdependent selves. Deirdre's heart and mind and spirit are so evident throughout her work, and I wholeheartedly encourage you to invite her, through this book, to be a guide and companion on your healing journey.

—**David S. Elliott, Ph.D.,** Co-author of *Attachment Disturbances in Adults: Treatment for Comprehensive Repair*; former President, Rhode Island Psychological Association

Informed by compassion and infused with love and profound understanding, *Becoming Safely Embodied* is the book you want as you heal trauma. Fay, a leader in the field of [mind-body] trauma treatment and a survivor herself, offers mindfulness, embodiment, and parts work practices that are easy to follow.

—**Amy Weintraub,** Author of *Yoga Skills for Therapists* and *Yoga for Depression* and the forthcoming novel *Temple Dancer*

Becoming Safely Embodied is my go to book when working with trauma and dissociation. The skills in this book gently and skillfully help people become aware of when their past takes over their present. This awareness is life changing. *The Becoming Safely Embodied* skills provide the structure to help people find ways to stay in the present while having compassion leading to new pathways for their future. I strongly recommend *Becoming Safely Embodied* for people working with trauma; these are powerful skills on the journey to recovery.

—**Clodagh Dowling, Ph.D.,** Principal Clinical Psychologist and Clinical Lead: Trauma Programme at St. Patrick's University Hospital, Dublin, Ireland

Becoming Safely Embodied is a wonderfully written guide to a set of eminently accessible and practical skills that transform the lives of people as they recover from trauma. The *Becoming Safely Embodied* skills allow people to gently and wisely enter their internal world to reconnect to their bodies and minds so they can gradually move toward a new life. Deirdre Fay writes with great humanity, compassion, and understanding. Her work draws on her vast experience as a psychotherapist, combined with evidenced-based practice, to produce an invaluable volume to become safely embodied. It is highly recommended.

—**Gary O'Reilly, Ph.D.,** Director of Doctoral
Training in Clinical Psychology, School of Psychology,
University College Dublin.

Deirdre Fay not only gets to the heart of complex issues in the management of traumatic activation, but she is then able to present her core understanding in a clear and concise manner. The skills in this book are designed to lessen distress and to provide ways of coping with disturbing feelings from the past that can be evoked by the ever-ongoing vicissitudes of life. The straightforward presentation ensures that everything is practical and grounded, anchored in the body. The *Becoming Safely Embodied* skills offer a gentle but effective approach to self-regulation and healing.

—**Frank Corrigan, M.D., FRCPsych,** Co-editor *Neurobiology
and Treatment of Traumatic Dissociation:
Towards an Embodied Self*

Deirdre Fay has written an invaluable and transformational guide to healing from trauma. This book offers concrete, practical steps that make starting your own trauma recovery group feel possible and hopeful. You can feel Deirdre's deep care and thoughtfulness with each page.

—**Anne Hallward, M.D.,** Host and
Founder of Safe Space Radio

BECOMING
SAFELY
EMBODIED

A Guide to Organize Your Mind, Body and Heart to Feel Secure in the World

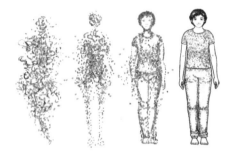

Deirdre Fay, MSW

FOREWORD BY

Janina Fisher, Ph.D.

Turn toward what nourishes you.
Live the life you want to live.

NEW YORK

LONDON • NASHVILLE • MELBOURNE • VANCOUVER

Becoming Safely Embodied

A Guide to Organize Your Mind, Body and Heart to Feel Secure in the World

Published in New York, New York, by Morgan James Publishing. Morgan James is a trademark of Morgan James, LLC. www.MorganJamesPublishing.com

This publication is designed to provide as accurate and authoritative information as possible regarding the subject matter covered. It is sold with the understanding that the publisher is not engaged in rendering psychological, financial, legal, or other professional services. If expert assistance or counseling is needed, the services of a competent professional should be sought.

From the author: "My intention in writing this book is to alleviate suffering. I'm glad to have you, the reader, use it for support on your healing path, and for those professionals in a helping field to assist your clients. Feel free to use the material for your personal or professional use, and attribute to: Becoming Safely Embodied by Deirdre Fay."

The author welcomes comments, feedback, and other correspondence. Her email address is: support@dfay.com

ISBN 9781631951848 paperback
ISBN 9781631951855 eBook
Library of Congress Control Number: 2020938081

Cover and Interior Design by:
Chris Treccani
www.3dogcreative.net

Second Edition Edited by:
Patrick Fay & vocem, LLC
With contributions from Jack Volpe Rotondi

Cover Illustration by:
Yuri Chen

Morgan James is a proud partner of Habitat for Humanity Peninsula and Greater Williamsburg. Partners in building since 2006.

Get involved today! Visit
MorganJamesPublishing.com/giving-back

With gratitude to all those who have shared their lives and struggles with me—thank you. You've inspired me, motivated me, and given me strength to find a way for all of us to keep trusting.

Together let's cultivate the world
we want to live in.

TABLE OF CONTENTS

ACKNOWLEDGMENTS

It's been a gift to reflect on the many people who have shaped and guided me on my personal and professional journey. Foremost are those I am unable to mention by name: my clients, who have been with me individually, in coaching groups, and in live and online courses. I have consistently been inspired by them as they've helped me learn better ways to implement these skills. Accompanying them on their healing journey has been a gift.

Many of these Becoming Safely Embodied (BSE) skills were formed in the cauldron of my six-and-a-half-year residency at a yoga ashram. Friends from that time have shaped my life. My sister, Sheila, and I lived there for much of the same time; I'm lucky to be blessed with a sister of integrity, honesty, and kindness. Thomas Amelio *(Shivanand)* introduced me to teachers and concepts that illuminated my consciousness. Anna Pool has been a true and loving friend over the years; Pat Sarley inspired me to live a life of consciousness.

I was also lucky to receive much of my meditation guidance at the hands of some incredible teachers. Sr. Kieran Flynn (Sisters of Mercy) first guided me through my early training in silent retreats and spiritual training. Michelle McDonald Smith and Sharon Salzberg taught me many intricacies of mindfulness and concentration practices. Jean Klein, the Advaita yogi, with his teachings and presence, pointed out the path of awareness. Under his guidance, I first learned to practice becoming safely embodied in my own body. Gehlek Rimpoche, the founder of Jewel Heart meditation, shaped my thinking and helped me advance my meditation practice. Dan Brown supported my mahamudra practice, as well as giving me a solid foundation in attachment theory, for which I'll always be grateful.

I was fortunate to work at the Trauma Center with Bessel van der Kolk who is one of the greatest visionaries in the field of trauma. We are all beneficiaries of his contributions to the field. Bessel had gathered a team of extraordinary therapists who created a generous, collaborative learning environment. Jodi Wigren, Sarah Stewart, Patti Levin, Kevin Becker, Deborah Korn, Jodie Wigren, Deborah Rozelle, Elizabeth Call, Richard Jacobs, Paula Morgan-Johnson, and Joanne Pomodoro contributed greatly to the team. Janina Fisher mentored me, supervised me, and befriended me. This book emerged out of her belief in the efficacy of my Becoming Safely Embodied (BSE) group approach that we subsequently co-led. I am indebted to her soft and gentle "nudges"—without which this book would never have taken form.

I am also grateful for my study and training in Yvonne Agazarian's group model, Systems Centered Therapy. Michael White, in his therapeutic approach of Narrative Therapy, was an early influence on my work. Nancy Napier generously helped me with the early conceptualization of this book. With a heart of appreciation, I'm grateful to Frank Corrigan, Chris Germer, Celia Grand, Rick Hanson, Liz Hall, Joan Klagsbrun, Jeri Schroeder, Paul Gilbert, Hannah Gilbert, and the whole Compassion Focused Therapy community. I was fortunate to be a faculty member at Pat Ogden's Sensorimotor Psychotherapy Institute in the early years.

I appreciate the careful editing of this book by Patrick Fay and Cortney Donelson and Sarah Greene at vocem, LLC. As for my work partner and husband, Jack Volpe Rotondi, who has helped me every step of the way, you enhance and nourish every facet of my life with love. Thank you!

I have been lucky to learn from teachers both gifted and profound. Whatever errors are contained in this book are simply the result of my continual grappling with the depth of this material.

FOREWORD

Traumatic experience affects not only our minds, emotions, and systems of belief, but also the body. At the moment of life threat, 'animal brain' instincts take precedence over reflective decision-making, allowing us to run, duck for cover, hide, fight back, or "huddle and wait for it to be over"—whatever best helps us to survive. Decades after the mind knows that we are safe, the body still responds as if it were under life threat. Triggered by everyday normal life stimuli directly or indirectly reminiscent of the trauma, the same bodily responses that originally helped us to survive are instinctively re-activated. What was once an adaptive survival response has now become a symptom. The body that used its animal brain instincts to negotiate a dangerous world now feels like an enemy, rather than an ally. It is ironic that the very same responses that *preserve* our physical and psychological integrity under threat also drive the symptoms of post-traumatic stress for months or years after the events themselves (van der Kolk et al, 1997; Ogden, Minton & Pain, 2006). To make matters more challenging, the survivor of trauma is left with a mind and body that now function better under conditions of threat than conditions of calm, peacefulness, or pleasure.

With the advent of technology that allows us to study the brain and nervous system responding to stimuli, researchers have observed that narrative memories of traumatic events are connected to intense states of autonomic nervous system arousal (van der Kolk & Fisler, 1995). Even "thinking about thinking about" the memories are often enough to cause a reactivation of the nervous system—as if the events were recurring right now, right here. Attempts to address the history of trauma through narrative therapy can quickly become complicated when the telling of the story evokes intense reactions that exacerbate the client's symptoms, rather than resolving them.

By the time the trauma survivor comes for group or individual treatment, the neurobiological and psychological effects of a hyper-activated nervous system and trauma-related emotional and attachment patterns have often become so well-entrenched and habitual that they now subjectively feel like "just who I am." The client has identified with the symptom, so that it is no longer the conveyor of a history that cannot be fully remembered or put into words: It is "me." In addition, other symptoms tend to have developed that represent valiant attempts to cope with the overwhelming physical and emotional experiences: self-injury and suicidality, shame and self-loathing, isolating, caretaking and self-sacrifice, re-victimization, and addictive behavior. All these patterns represent different ways of modulating a dysregulated nervous system: Self-injury and planning suicide induce adrenaline responses that increase feelings of calm and control; self-starvation and overeating each induce numbing; isolating allows avoidance of trauma-related stimuli; and addictive behaviors can induce either numbing or increased arousal (or a combination of both).

In traditional psychotherapy models, it has always been assumed that in re-telling the story and re-experiencing the feelings connected to what happened, these trauma responses would remit naturally on their own. Clinical experience and recent neurobiological research tell a different story: The human mind and nervous system will always tend to respond to a reminder of past threat as if it too were a threat, unless the brain's frontal cortex is "on line" and therefore able to discriminate a real threat from the reminder. To desensitize or transform a traumatic memory, we need to change the mind-body responses to that memory: to reinstate activity in the frontal lobes so we can interpret the responses differently or react to them differently. We need to counteract the habitual responses by calling attention to them, providing psychoeducation about how and why they are symptoms, encouraging mindfulness and curiosity in place of reactivity, pacing the exploration of the past so that the autonomic nervous system can be better regulated instead of dysregulated by the recovery process, and by encouraging the developing of new responses to triggers or memories that compete with the old habitual responses. We need to challenge the subjective perception of traumatized clients that the symptoms are just "who they are."

In 1998, when I first met Deirdre Fay as a colleague at the Trauma Center, an outpatient clinic and research center founded and directed by Bessel van der Kolk, she had been recently recruited as a staff member because of her many years of work in the yoga and mindfulness world. At that time, new research on the neuroscience of trauma had begun to yield findings that suggested that trauma treatment could not ignore the body in any form of effective treatment, and the Center needed a body specialist to help develop new approaches to trauma. When I first began sending clients to Deirdre Fay's "Becoming Safely Embodied" groups, I was simply hoping for the outcome all individual therapists do: that my clients find support and an opportunity to universalize their symptoms. I was unprepared for the immediate and dramatic changes in their capacity to engage in their individual therapies. Week after week, I observed that clients who were participating in the group were making gains at a rate far exceeding that of others. The client with whom I had talked ad infinitum about enmeshment with her nuclear family suddenly "got it" after a group focusing on boundaries using an experiential, rather than cognitive, approach. A client with a very long, painful history of early parental and sibling loss found unexpected comfort in a group devoted to the topic of belonging. A childlike, helplessly angry client developed skills that she began to use to modulate intense emotional and autonomic states, rather than drowning in them.

In ensuing years, I had the opportunity to learn the Becoming Safely Embodied model personally as a co-therapist in groups led by Deirdre Fay. As a result, I could come to appreciate the simplicity and creativity of this approach, and eventually urged Deirdre to publish her work so that it could be made available to other therapists and clients around the world. Deceptively simple, the model takes the essential ingredients of a trauma recovery program and breaks them down into small, achievable steps. Practice in mindful observation is needed, for instance, to challenge the automatic unthinking instinctual responses to traumatic triggers. Deliberate focus on cultivation of a sense of belonging can challenge habitual beliefs, such as "I don't belong" or "I don't matter to anyone." Cultivating the ability to step back from overwhelming experience to study its components (thoughts, feelings, and body sensations) is essential to the skill of modulating autonomic activation. Identifying facts versus feelings and learning how to be "present in the present" help cultivate past-present differentiation. Without the ability to make those discriminations, clients continue to feel a sense of unending subjection to threat for decades after the traumatic events are over. Finally, learning to deliberately choose new responses or deliberately change one's perspective challenges beliefs that nothing will ever change, that the survivor is helpless in the face of the intense activation, overwhelming emotions, and beliefs that she is damaged and defective. I can still recall a client whose pessimism and conviction of her own and others' defects were suddenly transformed by the instruction to tell the same story from two different perspectives. One was the perspective I had come to anticipate: angry, bitter, hopeless, and painfully lonely. But the next story suddenly allowed her access to another world of possibilities; it was the same narrative told in an affirming, tender, emotionally moving way and filled with faith in the world of human beings. Without the experience of that exercise, she would still be expecting *the* worst, and the therapist would still be expecting *her* worst.

Janina Fisher, Ph.D.
Oakland, California

MOTIVATION

The ancient wisdom traditions across all cultures invite us to have a clear motivation when we start a project or meditation. Since my work integrates contemplative practices, attachment theory, yogic psychology and trauma, it's fitting to share my motivation with you for developing these skills and for writing this book.

I'm interested in how we become solid, steady, and secure inside our own body, mind, and heart. What motivates me is finding simple, practical skills for people to live a full, rich, satisfying life inside their skin—connected to others and the world they live in.

INTRODUCTION TO
Becoming Safely Embodied

The mirror reflected back a person. It always had. That day, decades ago, was different somehow. I was in the gym, working out—something I always enjoyed. But this day, I looked in the mirror and realized, that's me. It was the oddest experience of realizing there was someone living inside my skin. I was used to working out, developing strength and flexibility, yet somehow, I hadn't connected to the being that was inside me.

As much work as I had done on myself, I came to realize I wasn't inhabiting my whole body-mind-heart. That revelation came in the late 1980s as my own trauma history erupted while I was living in a yoga ashram. I went from being able to meditate, practice yoga, and train for triathlons to, what seemed like overnight, unable to get out of bed or do the teaching I had done before with ease. How had I gone from experiencing my body as a temple for the soul . . . to living in inner chaos, confusion, and pretty constant distress? To answer that, I went back to the basics, integrating yoga, meditation, and the awareness of being in the body.

This book—which has its origins in my own experience, then developed further through groups I led in inpatient hospital settings, the Trauma Center, and private practice—introduces you to that approach.

The Becoming Safely Embodied (BSE) skills were developed on an integrated platform of spiritual practice and psychology. For forty years I have practiced yoga and meditation, and for thirty-five years I have trained in and practiced psychotherapy—including gestalt, systems-centered practice, Sensorimotor Psychotherapy, and Internal Family Systems. My experience with these approaches, each uniquely addressing health and wholeness, were the primary resources used in my own healing. They have been the mainstays of my work in helping others heal from their trauma.

During my training I applied these practices and skills to those on a dissociative unit at a major teaching hospital. The staff had heard about my years practicing and living a yogic/meditation lifestyle. They were curious if meditation and yoga could be helpful. In the evenings, after my shift was done, I would be with those on the unit, exploring what helped. In the process I learned how much I needed to scaffold (Lyons-Ruth) down the concepts to make them accessible. I'm grateful for my time with the people who were there.

Developing the BSE skills has also involved research with other long-term meditation and yoga practitioners. After living and working for six years in a yoga ashram, I became curious about what had happened to long-term yogis whose trauma histories came up while they participated in intensive spiritual practices. I wondered if their spiritual practices made it easier for them to be in their bodies. Did having a spiritual framework make healing trauma easier, even when the process was incredibly difficult? And if it did, could modern psychotherapeutic principles be successfully integrated with this other dimension of apparently deep healing practice, to form a clear, step-by-step approach to recover from trauma?

Translating and applying what I learned as a result of this inquiry with others became the basis for the modules contained in this book. Long-term meditators repeatedly told me they needed both psychotherapy as well as the meditation practices they were immersed in to help their healing. That was true for me as well. Despite the years of spiritual practice, I needed solid trauma treatment to weather the internal storms. As I have continually developed my own meditation and yoga practices, I have been able to discover a deep wisdom of the body/heart/mind, which has effectively served as an antidote to feelings of despair and resignation, reorienting toward a life of wellbeing, equanimity, and compassion.

In my own practice with individuals I realized I needed ways to help people organize the confusing life they were in, to make sense of it, all while growing, developing and flourishing. They would come to therapy one or two times a week, and then be alone for the other twenty-three hours a day, multiple days a week.

There were so many moments of being with someone as they stood on the threshold of our time together—the client knowing they had to leave, not wanting to go and be alone again. Those moments spurred me to find ways to support people during those many hours a day between therapy sessions. People who came to the BSE groups had good therapists. They were doing good work in therapy. Yet they needed more. They needed support being with their lives in between sessions. It was out of addressing that need that the BSE skills were born.

Throughout my years of working with trauma survivors and those with issues ranging from dissociation to attachment-wounding, and shame to stress, I have become increasingly moved by their deep longing to feel better, even amid frequent despair. Becoming Safely Embodied represents a structured yet flexible approach that has proven effective in both my personal and professional work.

In this book I refer to "trauma" as shorthand for a broader band of challenges many of us face. Research has shown that trauma is less likely to resolve when the underlying attachment wounds aren't addressed, because the body's felt experience is different from our understanding of what goes on there. Eugene Gendlin invited us into the "felt experience" of what happens inside. Daniel Stern wrote of the "vibrational affects" and body therapists like Susan Aposhyan speak of the "pulsatory energy." When there's been trauma, people are often left confused by these internal signals of energy, often fearing what happens as they are hijacked and catapulted into distress.

Over time, working with people in a variety of settings—those with PTSD, complex PTSD, dissociation—I found time and again that these skills helped them with a wide variety of emotional/psychological wounds. Broadly construed, BSE can help with issues ranging from trauma to dissociation to attachment-wounding to shame to stress and beyond. The BSE skills are a simple, practical, concrete way to do so.

After twenty years of leading BSE groups in person and online, I have witnessed thousands of people with trauma histories make longed-for changes and live the lives they always wanted to live. For some, practicing these BSE skills on their own can be a game changer, yet there are times—sometimes prolonged, when individual therapy is essential. Having a trusted therapist skilled at the many layers of psychological healing makes all the difference. Individual therapy provides the space and holding environment to listen deeply—allowing the wounded, exiled parts to emerge—which may not be possible in regular, day to day life.

In life, having structure to be able to dip into those old wounded places, and then dipping out, coming out for air helps healing to be balanced and manageable.

Overall, welcoming all of our parts, all of our experiences, and creating room inside to have an Unshakeable Core happens through multiple disciplines.

As I repeat to others (and to myself!) there is no right way to do this. The good thing is, there is also no wrong way to do it. We need to become skillful, adapting to different circumstances, having multiple modalities in our toolbox. I'm hoping the BSE skills become some of the many tools you use in having the life you want to live.

Learning these skills does not depend on having or developing a spiritual perspective. Nevertheless, these skills serve as an invitation to encounter what the body knows and for what the heart yearns.

Having now taught the Becoming Safely Embodied online skills course for decades, and having had another cohort of professionals recently become certified in these simple tools, I'm grateful for how the BSE skills ripple into the world.

Over and over throughout the years people find the BSE skills help make their inner world more understandable and accessible. With practice, they find themselves transforming old painful patterns into nourishing life-sustaining ways of living.

Dive in. Try one. See what changes. Something will open up. Let yourself be surprised at what you'll find. Becoming Safely Embodied helps you become more aware of what works in you and what you'd like to change.

Our Bodies are the Temples of Our Souls

The ancient wisdom traditions invite us into the body, which shelters our heart, opening the door to our soul. In yoga and many other spiritual traditions, the body is considered the temple of the soul. Yoga psychology suggests there are many layers of the body, *koshas,* which provide access points to different ways of knowing. My training in different mystical traditions highlights the importance of the heart, and the layers of the heart, contained within the body.

The promise is there—inviting us. Yet many trauma survivors can't begin to imagine their bodies as safe, let alone sacred, thereby denying themselves the experience of living a safely embodied life. Their internal world is often chaotic and horrific, and their bodies repositories of great anguish and pain. A trauma survivor might easily describe their body not as a temple but instead as a desecrated, scorched earth.

Our challenges include: healing our inner worlds, integrating our native movement toward compassion and possibility, bringing in curiosity, welcoming the steps that take our body from feeling unsafe or confusing to living inside our own skin, and opening to the wisdom that naturally flows through us.

Becoming Safely Embodied comes as we integrate the outside world with our inside world. There are two main axes, which provide this integration, bringing wholeness. When we're connecting with people, events, circumstances in life outside of ourselves, we're connecting on our Horizontal Axis. Our relationships with life bridge the outside world with our inner world. That external connection joins us through our bodies, providing a way to integrate within ourselves.

We also have a Vertical Axis connecting our psychological self with our sensory body—with our heart experience—opening the door to our inner wisdom and ultimately to connections through the earth into the holy expressions of grounded native wisdom as well as flowing up through the channel of the body accessing the sacred unity of the Divine. In this perspective, our heart is the connection between the vertical and the horizontal.

In my professional practice I found it helpful to not only see clients individually, but to also provide a well mapped out approach with step-by-step suggestions that they could do on their own. There are so many, many hours in a day, in a week, when someone suffering from trauma is alone, grappling with the mess of it all. My goal with this book is to use what's worked for individuals and groups to help you have a similar way to "becoming safely embodied." This guidebook, then, includes small manageable steps—allowing you to gently open the door to your internal world, and to safely begin making distinctions between what's happening *now* and what happened in the past. This will allow you to listen to the inner wisdom that wants to guide you home to yourself.

The BSE system acts as both a map and guidebook. This book presents the nine core skills that can help you to be more at home with your internal world, cultivate a body that's a safe place for rest, reflection, and wellbeing, and take steps to create the life you want to live, instead of living in the life your history catapults you into.

If you are an individual on your own healing path and are interested in using these skills in a deeper way, there is a wealth of opportunity to learn, grow, and flourish using the Becoming Safely Embodied skills. There have been many people who have shared their stories throughout the years of picking up this book and trying just one thing, finding that one thing made all the difference. It's something we consistently hear from those who have read this book, taken the Becoming Safely Embodied online skills course, or joined our groups.

Want to hear some inspiring stories or explore additional free resources? I'd love to share them with you . . . so I've created a special resources section online!

To access the FREE online book bonuses type
the following link into a web browser:
dfay.com/resources

A note about working with clients and groups: If you are a professional in a helping field and are interested in using these skills with your clients in a deeper way, please contact support@dfay.com to learn more about my professional certification programs. To explore a variety of free resources for you as a helping professional (including group-oriented handouts), as well as other resources helpful on your own personal healing path, go to: dfay.com/resources

Group work can be especially healing for anyone who has emotionally isolated themselves or feels no one could possibly understand their experience(s). In the Safely Embodied Network people discover they are not alone, that they can and do learn from others, and they support each other. It's a joy to see people share their experience(s) with the group and realize they are contributing to someone else's healing. What they have learned becomes a gift offered, as well as one received. In this way, the groups are part of the larger Safely Embodied Network community and become a vital repository of connection, belonging, and collective wisdom. I am astounded at how a felt experience of belonging and safety has been established in all our online courses, groups, and retreats.

PART I
Setting the Foundation

PRINCIPLES OF BECOMING
SAFELY EMBODIED

Before presenting the nine skill sets in depth, I want to introduce the major principles that underlie the series.

Practice: It's essential to practice what we hope to learn. When you practice BSE, the skills become more familiar and easier to remember. Eventually they become a new habit, embodied, and begin to replace old dysfunctional ways of being. I've set up each skill section with a practice component. This portion is especially important, as this is where you take the learning and access your own wisdom.

Journal and Community: Having a journal where you watch the changes take place gives a tangible way of remembering why you're doing this! It supports your courage, validates your determination, and offers you hope and encouragement as you see shifts along the way. It's also important to find positive communities of people to help you shift old patterns. People can find that in church groups, yoga or exercise classes, and online groups. The most important part is to find communities that create safety for you and the others in it.

Coming out of isolation and separation is, in and of itself, healing: One of the most inspiring experiences I've had sharing these skills with people throughout the years has been to watch people listen to their own hearts, trusting their own knowing. This is the gift of practicing with others. When people practice with others who have similar backgrounds, they discover they are not alone. They experience kinship. When I teach groups live (online or in person), people learn from each other, and their learning, in turn, supports the healing of others through their struggles and their triumphs. Holding strong common intentions, we become a community of support and authentic inquiry. Certainly, we'd welcome you to join us as well! If you want further support as you go through this, consider joining the Safely Embodied Learning Community (SELC) to help integrate these practices with the support of other like-hearted people. To discover how to join the SELC community online, go to this link: dfay.com/SELC

Safety exists when you are present: The key to healing is training ourselves to live in this present moment. When the past intrudes—when our trauma intrudes—we are caught in spirals of fear, uncertainty, depression, and shame. One of the vital learnings of *Becoming Safely Embodied* is separating out the past from the present. When we land here, now, in this moment, we can find safety. When we're here, the entire weight of our histories and the unknown nature of the future is not constantly bearing down on us. Life becomes more manageable. Once we can trust being inside our own skin or being aware of our shifting thoughts, feelings, and sensations (T/F/S), we encounter a positive feedback loop that we can befriend.

Meditation practice provides two foundational skills that are useful in navigating the internal world: mindfulness and concentration. Both practices receive further treatment in the section on meditation in this book. Mindfulness trains us to notice, without judgment, whereas concentration practices develop a capacity to focus where we want our attention to go and hold it there. This skill is particularly critical for trauma survivors.

Handling flashbacks is an example of concentration's usefulness. When you can concentrate on something in the present (such as your breathing or the sensory experience of seeing or touching something), you may be able to stem the threatening tide of dysregulation when a flashback pulls you toward the emotional experience of earlier trauma.

For many, having a spiritual framework helps immensely: There is no logical understanding or reason for all the pain and suffering people endure in this world. Exploring the possibility of an integrative universal force can help hold the suffering and support a cosmological framework. Accessing the clear, wise, trustworthy impulses and instincts within us can serve as an antidote to despair and build a sense of strength and realistic hope.

There is no way to do this wrong: This is a cornerstone point of view, a mantra we can repeat over and over again! There is no right way. And there is no wrong way. "Mistakes" are ways to learn, grow, develop, and become. Mistakes are, in fact, essential . . . the mud out of which wisdom grows. They help us cultivate an attitude of self-compassion. Something happened. It didn't work out how we wanted. Welcoming those moments with self-compassion, we develop an internal ecosystem to experience our lives differently. Mistakes arise as wisdom.

Feel free to experiment by modifying strategies and directions, depending on what works for you. There is no grading system, and no one is expected to get the outcome "right." There is no "wrong." There is just pure exploration. Develop curiosity in the process . . . discover that your internal world is interesting and compelling. Yes, there's pain and distress. But there's also a lot more. If we only focus on what's wrong, what hurts, the pain that we're in, we'll also miss the calm, ease, and sparkling vibrancy that animates our experience as well. This is an opportunity to let yourself be surprised—and delighted—by what comes forward.

Use the BSE skills to see what happens. Encourage curiosity as you open doors to your inner world.

SIMPLE BREATHING PRACTICES
THAT HELP

The breath can be an emotional regulator. It's why many people unconsciously control their breath. When we are shocked with something, there's a quick inhalation or a pause—it's almost like we're stopping the moment as a way to integrate it. Often, though, whatever information is coming in from outside, or bubbling up from inside, isn't easily integrated. Those habitual ways of being become automatic.

As we're looking to find more satisfying ways to be in our body, becoming curious makes a huge difference. When we're experiencing something new or intense, we can become blinded by our fear of the unknown. Learning to stay open and becoming curious in those situations allows us to explore what's happening and to learn from it. This is certainly true about breathing.

You may have heard the suggestion to take deep breaths. This can be difficult because when you take full, deep breaths you can expand the range and/or intensity of what you are feeling—which may be exactly what you don't want to happen!

Certain breathing patterns are better for calming; others for energizing. Experiment with these breathing techniques to see what happens. I'm including a few of the many ways to befriend the breath that flows in and through your body. If at any time you feel uncomfortable or dizzy, immediately breathe normally and rest for a few minutes before more gently exploring again.

Little sips of breath: Deep breathing is conducive to moving the body's inner energy, so you may prefer to take little breaths to oxygenate your lungs without disturbing your internal state. Take a sip of breath, rather than a deep draught. Gently let the breath out. Pause and notice what happens. When it feels right take another sip of breath. Notice that if you take small sips of breath in a rapid way you may hyperventilate. That's not what we want! Instead take a small sip of breath, noticing what happens inside, then take another, and another.

Controlled breathing: Take a breath in for five beats, letting your belly expand. Then exhale slowly to the count of five. People in the BSE groups consistently report being able to calm themselves; for some, it's a way to ease into sleep. Research has shown controlled breathing to reduce stress, anxiety, insomnia, PTSD, depression, attention deficit disorder, increase alertness, and boost the immune system. Richard Brown, M.D. and Patricia Gerbarg, M.D. explore this in their book, *The Healing Power of Breath.* When we consciously change our breath pattern, we appear to be sending signals to the brain to adjust the parasympathetic branch of the nervous system, which slows our heart rate and digestion, while also calming the sympathetic system which generates the release of stress hormones.

Kumbach: Yogis practice various breathing techniques. Indeed, Pranayama, "breath control" or "breath liberation," is one of the eight "limbs" of yoga. Kumbach is the practice of holding one's breath as you inhale or as you exhale. When you feel anxious, try breathing in and holding your breath for a second or two, whatever feels comfortable. Then, exhale softly and slowly, gently and briefly pausing at the end of your exhale before taking another breath. Be aware that too many cycles could intensify your experience, instead of calming you. Start with one in-and-out cycle, breathing normally in and out, with the pauses I mentioned, and see how you feel. If you're comfortable, try again: breathing in, holding, exhaling, and then pausing on the exhale for a beat or two before inhaling again. Some people find it helpful to only hold/pause on the inhalation, or only the exhalation. See what works for you.

Three-part breath: Imagine filling your lungs completely. Begin with a deep, steady-but-slow inhalation—so deep that your belly gradually enlarges. This does not involve force; it's a matter of opening and allowing. Exhale naturally. When you next breathe into your belly, breathe in until you feel your belly and chest expand. Exhale. On the third try, breathe fully into the collarbone area too. Try this again, but reverse the order as you focus on exhaling—first exhale from the collarbone area, then from your chest, before releasing the air out from your stomach area. Think of it as emptying a glass. Practice this approach for a few cycles.

Relaxing the body: When we get upset, our muscles tighten and contract. Letting go of that tension allows us to relax more fully. But for trauma victims, relaxing may feel dangerous. Try letting your body relax when you are in a safe place and invite yourself to mindfully experience what's happening in the moment, rather than closing yourself off. Use your breath to stay focused on the here and now; in this way, you learn to observe your experience, rather than identify with it. Go slowly.

DISCRIMINATING INNER EXPERIENCE

What do you notice when you focus your attention inside yourself?

What kind of experience are you having at that moment?

What's the main thing you notice? Thoughts, feelings, or body sensations?

You might not know if you're not yet able to distinguish one sensation or feeling from another. In time, you will, as you differentiate the various internal states. Right now, just notice what's happening for you *without trying to change anything*.

It's often helpful to start a journal and record your insights. A journal can also serve as a diary of your journey toward self-healing.

To help you slow the process down even more, and help you not be overwhelmed, try externalizing, noticing/naming, and dis-identifying.

Externalizing

Often so much is going on inside, it is hard to define each internal experience. It may help to externalize overwhelming material—that is, to imagine what you feel inside and project it outside of yourself. Give it a name, a shape, or a character. Dialogue with that part of yourself. Describe or draw that aspect of your experience. This may help you stay in touch with your experience rather than getting lost in it.

Noticing and Naming

We aren't always aware of what is going on inside or outside us. For example, as we cross a street, we might be so caught up in our inner experience that we fail to notice the pedestrian signal changing, the people around us, the scent of fall leaves, or the touch of a soft breeze. Sometimes we just space out. Practicing awareness opens us up to what is—inside and out. Try it out. Notice what's going on around you right now, but don't get caught up in a story about it. *Just notice, name, and let go.*

Dis-identifying

Practicing naming what is there allows us to be more fully aware of an experience without getting caught up in it. Dis-identifying from something is different from dissociating from it. When we dissociate, we leave ourselves behind; dis-identifying from something reminds us that we are present, connected in our experience, with the space not to be overwhelmed or needing to shut down.

Catching yourself unaware is already a victory! I can't stress this enough. So what if you were spacing out or obsessing about something? Now is the perfect time to start noticing what you were filtering out of awareness. "Coming back" to awareness is all it takes.

A Note About Drawing

You may think you're not an artist and can't imagine drawing anything! I get that a lot from people in my groups, workshops, and trainings. To draw or represent something internal in a nonverbal way may feel daunting at first. You'll be accessing a different part of the brain.

Here's an easy way to start. Sense something inside your body. Without analyzing to much, simply imagine what color and shape seems to represent that something. Remember, there's no right way to do this. There's no wrong way. In fact, you can't fail at this. What if you were to take that internal representation, and, however awkwardly or easily, represent it on paper?

HARNESSING AND DIRECTING YOUR ENERGY

Attention and Noticing

Once we become aware of where our attention is—noticing what we're paying attention to—we can make changes. It's hard to change when we don't notice what's going on or can't pinpoint what is happening. We become empowered when we intentionally direct our energy and attention for our own learning and healing. We're no longer trapped . . . caught in an experience we don't want to have.

Compassion

To shift from our negative mind states, most of us need to cultivate compassion for ourselves and for others. Unfortunately, the external world we live in, and often our internal experience, is inundated with harsh criticism and judgment. Caring and kindness may be in short supply. Since these qualities tend to be overlooked, give yourself a high-five every time you embrace them. (To find out more about compassion, explore the work of Paul Gilbert and his colleagues. To deepen your self-compassion practice, access the practices and training of Mindful Self-Compassion developed by Kristin Neff & Christopher Germer.)

Practice: Healing is an Olympian Endeavor

If you're anything like me, you'll want everything to be changed instantly, including yourself! Yet, it's only through frequent practice that any of us can master basic skills. Practicing when we're less triggered helps carve new pathways in our brain and nervous system. The more we practice, the more habitual and automatic . . . the more the skills are there when we need them most. I wish there was a short cut! I haven't found it yet after searching for many years.

I've often wished we had an Olympic Medal for Healing. Like any Olympian endeavor, healing takes enormous practice, development of skills, training our body, mind, and heart to accomplish a task. In our case, with the BSE skills, it's to integrate what feels fragmented and disorganized inside.

Which is why we need to practice, practice, practice.

As you practice, you'll likely notice yourself developing a stronger observing capacity, meaning you'll be less reactive, more able to respond in ways that feel attuned to who you want to be. This will eventually allow you to choose the experiences you want to have, instead of feeling like you must "make do" with whatever patterns are in place now.

This happens as you begin to distinguish the building blocks of experience so you can see how you can intervene when older stuck patterns start to intrude.

You'll discover what happens in your body when you're triggered and explore healing ways of effectively dealing with triggers.

One simple way you can start is to look for the differences in apparent similarities. It's something I learned from Yvonne Agazarian's Living Human Systems approach. Even with many similarities, we are not the same. We often learn the hard way that others think, speak, feel, or perceive life differently than we do. By looking for where things are different, even though they appear to be similar, we can discover new ways of being with ourselves—and with others.

Mirroring this, consider the idea of common humanity that is key to the Mindful Self-Compassion work of Kristin Neff and Christopher Germer. It's helpful to keep in mind that the person(s) across from you *is/are* different. Their differences may include gender identity, sexual preference, race, religion, cultural heritage, family background, trauma history, and hundreds of other areas of diversity. Yet, even with that, how are we similar?

If you find yourself getting triggered by others, try looking for non-negative, non-triggering reasons for their behavior. As we venture further into this book, you'll see that our bodies react as the past intrudes into our present, but that doesn't mean you have to act out of old patterns. Instead, we can practice staying in the present moment while noticing how our bodies are responding.

Access a simple video titled "Change Only Happens in This Moment" in the free online book bonuses at dfay.com/resources.

Easy ways to practice this can be to:

1. Pause before speaking. Ground yourself in your spine or your heart. From that place, speak about yourself and what is going on for you.
   "I feel . . . "
   "When I observe . . . (this), I feel . . . (this) . . . "
2. Notice your reactions/impulses. Is there something you want to move away from? If you slow the reaction or impulse down, is there something you're needing and wanting that gives rise to the reaction or impulse?
3. Explore *your* experience rather than other people's experiences. Before reacting and speaking out about another's issue, notice what you might be

experiencing inside yourself. Is there a way to speak that shares your experience instead?

4. Ask permission from others before giving advice or touching them. Keep in mind that others may not be experiencing life the same way that you do—at least not in that moment. As much as you can, speak respectfully and consciously. People may, or may not, be comforted by your genuine, spontaneous touch or advice. Asking their permission, and truly pausing as they consider, allows the other person the choice to receive the spontaneity in the spirit you have intended.

PROTEST AS OUR SECRET GUIDANCE SYSTEM

As I've integrated the theory of attachment, which is the understanding of how relationships with others and with ourselves affect us throughout our lives, I've found the research of John Bowlby (who we can consider the grandfather of attachment theory) and James Robertson illuminating. They studied what happened to children who were removed from their parents. What they found was that children seemed to go through three phases of separation distress.

The first phase is an active form of PROTEST! Children wail and stomp and express their fury. They may actively keep seeking connection with the caregiver, looking out of windows, running to the door. When the parent returns, the child can let the parent know through behavior and words how difficult a time it was, but will then be able to settle back into connection.

If the separation continues longer, the child will move into a phase they called DESPAIR. The active protesting comes to a close; instead, the child withdraws, droops, and becomes miserable—appearing to lose interest in their surroundings and the people in it. This isn't about "settling in," but rather a painful shutting off of experience.

Protest didn't work and despair takes over.

The third phase is one of DETACHMENT, where the child can appear to interact with others but when the parent arrives back in the scene, the child will seem to not recognize or care, acting as though they didn't need any parenting at all. This third phase is the most problematic. It's as though the child has shut off the love they had—the need they had for the connection. As Bowlby and Robertson showed, the connections they now have are more superficial and emotionally distant.

Becoming Safely Embodied takes these three phases, calling them all PROTEST as a way to describe the normal and natural protections that come when we step outside our comfort zone. If we haven't had a safe way to connect with ourselves, then fears, resistances, and blocks arise. These are perfect times to welcome in what's uncomfortable—slowing down the process—to befriend what's there. It reminds me of what Carl Jung would tell his students: "We have nightmares because we haven't gotten to know our nightly dreams."

Encountering protest happens every day. We might be annoyed that we overslept, irritated when our Internet freezes, or feel the shock of someone's rejection.

We may even protest when someone says something good to us; protest happens on a deep and wide spectrum.

These simple forms of protest are ones we can welcome as guideposts to point us in a new direction. When we enter new situations, we may feel self-conscious, or unsure of what's happening. We might get overwhelmed, or realize we can't think clearly. That's okay. Whatever happens is okay. The steps outlined in this book are ways to settle in—to take notice of our thoughts, feelings, and sensations without judgment. There is neither a right way nor a wrong way to do this.

Whatever we're protesting is something we make very clear: "It shouldn't be this way!!" On the heels of that is the wish for "it" to be different. In some small way that happened when you acquired this book. There's something you want to be different. That protest has an inherent unmet need in it. You're looking for some help in finding a way to meet that need. Your hope, and my sincere desire, is to help you meet that need, thereby shifting the protest.

Take a moment to find a bit of quiet. Consider what drew you to this book? Was it the title? The idea of becoming safely embodied? Because what inside you is wanting your life—your experience—to be different?

_____

_____

_____

_____

_____

That intention—that wish for life to be different—is the flame you want to kindle. Something deep inside you knows something. You have a sense that something should be different than what it is. That sense doesn't have to be the "right" thing, nor a single intention . . . try this out:

As you tune into your own inner connection you might first find yourself protesting. You might have voices (or parts) annoyed, irritated, angry, judgmental, surprised, and resistant . . . Getting to know our protest is an important first step!

Take a moment and welcome them. I'm curious what happens as you do so? What happens as you let those voices/parts of you know that you get that they're protesting? They're trying to get your attention for a reason. They're pushing against something (protesting) because they need something they haven't gotten.

What do we say when we're protesting something?

"It shouldn't be like this!" or "This isn't RIGHT!!!" or "This is NOT fair!!!" We all have some version of protest that takes over. It might be to criticize, get angry, judge, or blame. Do you have a sense of what your "favorite version" is? What do you tend to do and say?

In my twenties, I watched myself in some way, shape, or form blame someone else for whatever happened that I didn't like. Sheepishly, I began to recognize that as a form of protest—orienting me to something missing.

I often tell my training groups that our bodies, our minds, and our hearts are protesting because we know something should be different. Protest, instead of being something bad, is actually our secret inner guidance system—if we're paying attention.

Foundational Attachment Needs

Part of the reason our protest can be intense is because it is linked to old unmet needs. Some of these are so primary that we are used to pushing the protest aside. Through my work with my attachment mentor, Daniel Brown, PhD, I realized there were seven Foundational Attachment Needs we all have. When we don't have those needs met, we feel "needy"—we feel the horrible awful feeling of being exposed. In fact, I often think of shame as an attachment wound. When we don't get what we need—when we don't get these very normal and natural needs met— we feel there is something fundamentally wrong with us.

Let's make this practical. When a child is crying, raising her arms—she wants something. Most basically, she wants to be picked up, to be close, to be reassured, comforted, fed, changed, and the like. So normal, right? Sitting with that in my own body, I realized that process isn't just physical. Or maybe a better way to say it is that accompanying the physical gesture is usually some of kind "attachment cry," or unspoken need. The physical movements were an indication of something else—some need the child has, needs we all have. Naming these needs are absolutely normal to every one of us. Everyone has them! We can't escape them, even though we try to deny them.

This is our common humanity. We all share these primary basic needs—to form a secure attachment. Now let's tie in how these fundamental needs fit into Becoming Safely Embodied.

One of the most basic needs we all have is to have an adequate amount of protection and good enough physical, emotional, or psychological care. If we get these, we'll have a felt sense of safety.

When somebody attunes to us, we feel gotten—we feel seen and known.

When we're scared or worried or anxious, and somebody is there to reassure us and soothe us, well, then our body has a felt sense of calm. And through this, we develop the capacity to regulate our emotions.

When somebody expresses delight in us, we develop pride and self-worth.

If we're guided and mentored, an urge to become who we are—not the expression of somebody else—then we develop trust in ourselves and in our motivations. And we learn that mistakes aren't there to shame us or humiliate us, but to course correct and guide us.

Another essential need we all have is to know that conflict does not have to be disastrous, but it can be repaired, and that it's out of conflict that relationships actually get stronger. Isn't that a new concept for most of us! And yet, our body knows this to be true. Our heart hurts when there's conflict. Why? We know there should be connection—should be a way to be close and separate at the same time. We long for repair. For things to be better.

Finally, what we need evoked in our lives and relationships is to have a sense of ease and fluidity, of knowing we don't have to take things personally—that all is well. This points us in the direction of wellbeing.

These seven fundamental attachment needs are absolutely hardwired. Every human being has these needs, and we all want to have these basic needs met. When we do get these needs met, we develop this inner ground—a secure base. Even if we don't have these needs met as a child, we can earn them as an adult.

And for that to happen, Bowlby said we need to have an older, wiser person. Now, it doesn't have to be somebody that's much older (and they don't have to be that much wiser!), but we need somebody who is a little bit ahead of us on the path—someone who can show us the way. It might be a coach or a teacher, an elder in the community, another family member—someone who's there who makes it safe to step out into the world, to explore, and inquire. I'm hoping this book will provide that kind of guide in your Becoming Safely Embodied.

Setting Intentions

Does that help you settle into your experience? Perhaps giving you room to welcome what's happening in you? Remember, it is possible to shift the patterns that run our lives. They are the background assumptions out of which we live. Yet, we are not stuck to them; we can shift and choose ones that serve us better.

It's always important to take a moment before starting something new to set an intention for what you'd like this new experience to bring. When we take the time to set an active intention we interact with our patterns—our old habits—and create a crack in the door, allowing fresh air to come in and the possibility of a new way of being.

A working definition for intention could be to have in mind a purpose or plan, to direct ourselves toward—to have something we're aiming toward. Without an intention we are often pushed and pulled by whatever is there in the moment. Ever have this experience? Say you're surfing the web . . . following one thread . . . and, before you know it, you're way off track. (It can happen way too many times for some of us!)

We also need to pay attention to the difference between goals and intentions. Goals are usually external outcomes that we want to happen in the future. Usually we meet our goals through planning, discipline, and changing our behavior. Goals can provide important measures we pay attention to at different times in our life.

Intentions, on the other hand, are what we hope for in the present moment—a practice we are engaging in to focus on at this moment in time. We set intentions based on what is important to us—what matters to us—and then align our outer world in accordance with these inner values. Our intentions inform each moment, keeping us close to our heart's wishes, and moving us on the path toward our external goals.

If you'd like to listen to me guide you through a free meditation on Setting Intentions, one that is included in the paid version of the Becoming Safely Embodied online course, I'm including it as part of the free bonuses for this book: dfay.com/resources

STAYING IN THE HERE AND NOW

Relax

When we get upset, our muscles contract and tighten; that's our body's attempt to contain the experience that feels "threatening" or new. Notice where the tension is in your body and invite that area to relax. Letting your body relax, the muscles around the tension can slowly allow you to experience underlying sensations, rather than remain guarded against them.

We tend to think, especially if we have a trauma history, that if we relax life will be filled with more of the overwhelming stuff. Some people manage this by hoping to disappear and get out of the way; others manage it by becoming forceful and strong, trying to project an image of invulnerability. As we learn to relax our muscles and create more inner space, the internal agitation will subside.

To get a sense of where you are now, notice how your body responds when you suggest the tension relax?

Slow Down—Body Time

When we enter states of over-arousal, over-stimulation, hypersensitivity, or any other related states that we all know so well, it is often because we haven't learned to slow ourselves down or taken the time to become keen observers. Instead, it is as if we've abdicated control over the process or taken our hands off the steering wheel.

Slowing down reminds us that no experience takes us from zero to sixty without first moving from one, two, three, four, all the way up to fifty-seven, fifty-eight, fifty-nine, and finally sixty. As we learn to slow down our inner state, we learn to stay with ourselves amid our experiences. We can more easily see where we have choices. It's not an out-of-control escalator . . . instead, it's a conscious, gentle step by step.

It's hard to slow down when our physiology is triggered and we feel out of control. Getting triggered happens when some unfinished piece of your history gets activated in your current moment. You might feel overwhelmed, go numb, or feel spaced out; life might feel too big or you may feel like you're in the middle of a storm or explosion. At those times, you can assume you are dealing with triggered experiences from the past. (We'll go into this more in subsequent chapters.)

Slowing down brings us to the place of taking charge of life instead of being subsumed into whatever life is dishing out. The more we practice slowing down, the easier it is.

Pause for a moment. Take a breath. Let whatever is happening happen without your doing anything. Take a pulse of how you are in this moment; this will be helpful for you to remember as you go through the rest of the practices.

Become Fascinated

So often when we're facing something new, we can become blinded by our fear of the unknown. Learning to stay open and become fascinated by new experiences creates space inside of ourselves to continue exploring. Along the way we find ourselves becoming more intrigued with our inner world and we can even start to fall in love with ourselves. This becomes even more important as we bear witness to our experiences when triggered.

Is it even possible to imagine becoming fascinated with the sequence of events that happen when you're triggered?

Notice

Once we learn to notice what is there, we have already begun the process of making space for ourselves. Noticing allows us to be the "see-er" (i.e., the one who is seeing), not the one who is at the mercy of unwanted experience. That simple act disengages us a bit from what is upsetting us and that defaults us into our habitual ways of interacting with life.

Often when we become overwhelmed, regressed, or filled with some emotional or physiological state, it is in part because *it* has taken over. We are no longer in charge of *it;* for *it* controls us. If we move too quickly, or if we allow the physiological state to hijack us without noticing how it happens, we will never learn how to apply the brakes. Ultimately, we lose ourselves in the process.

There are two steps to make the transition from outside to inside. The first one is to shift gears, turning our attention inside as we let go of attending to the outside world. This may be awkward in the beginning. You may find, as Ralph did (Editor's Note: all client names have been changed to ensure confidentiality), that even though his eyes were closed, his other senses were hyper-alert. It's important to notice if that happens. Appreciate how much you've had to always be on alert, monitoring what goes on outside you. Pause for a moment, offering yourself a bit of self-compassion for how hard it is.

The second step is to cross the inner threshold from your head to your heart. It's the transition from thinking about what's going on to being open to sensing what's in your heart. It can help to put a hand gently over your heart, breathing softly, and noting the warmth of your hand.

As you pause in this moment, what are you noticing as you become aware of your inner world? What makes it easier? What complicates it? Are you able to let go of any judgment about this? What is your experience of crossing the threshold as you turn your attention from outside to inside? And then from your head to your heart?

_____

_____

_____

_____

_____

If you want to use a guided meditation, feel free to use the free "Six Sides of the Breath" audio meditation in the free online book bonuses: dfay.com/resources

PART II
Skills in Action

BRIEF OVERVIEW OF SKILL SETS AND OBJECTIVES

Skill Set 1–Belonging

These practices allow us to find the invisible threads that bind us to our inner world, to others, and to the larger world. The practices can also support a developing awareness of something more essential and healing—a very real and benevolent holding environment that is at once accessible and completely profound.

Skill Set 2–Meditation

Although mindfulness and concentration practices are different, they both cultivate a means of being more present inside our bodies and minds.

- *Mindfulness skills* develop the observing ego and help with dis-identification from symptoms.
- *Concentration skills*—in this case, *metta* (loving kindness)—develop the capacity to focus and direct attention, as well as increase tolerance of inner conflict while fostering internal kindness.
- *Self-compassion and attachment in healing shame* are essential to healing as it provides a felt experience of transforming suffering.

Skill Set 3–Internal Information Flow

These exercises help you to differentiate more clearly between thoughts, feelings, and sensations. Developing these distinctions aids in slowing down experience—a useful and practical way to intervene in chaotic moments. These distinctions can also help resolve triggers through better recognition.

Skill Set 4–Separating Facts from Feelings

This part of the work elaborates on the previous module and encourages separation of brain functions (limbic from cortex). The goal is to ground you in the here and now, while providing containment for triggered material.

Skill Set 5–Addressing Parallel Lives

As you reinforce your ability to discern past from present, the distinction of having "parallel lives" draws psychological boundaries between the adult/wise part of self and those parts of the traumatized self that are triggered. This skill set can also assist in deconstructing and resolving triggers.

Skill Set 6–Working with Parts

Here is a chance to discover the basis of a solid self-structure from which you can quiet the internal cacophony, calm emotional dysregulation, and support communication between various parts of yourself.

Skill Set 7–Carving Out a New Path

Now we'll be creating a step-by-step roadmap for integrating previous skills: concentration, mindfulness, separating facts/feelings and past/present, recognizing triggers, and soothing parts. This skill helps you to start gathering evidence for the life you want to live, instead of reliving stuck, painful states of being.

Skill Set 8–Telling and Retelling

Through creative narratives, you can develop and refine new perspectives. Grounding those new perspectives in the body, and practicing a more empowered approach develops a playful approach to entrenched life situations.

Skill Set 9–Finding Guidance From Your Older, Wiser Self

Knowing there's a way through the horribly convoluted path of healing offers you a way to move from despair to hopefulness and supports perseverance for finding the way through. This section is about accessing our own inner wisdom that gently guides us through the bumps and falls of healing from trauma.

SKILL 1: BELONGING

Objectives

- To nurture a sense of belonging
- To offset isolation, loneliness, and alienation
- To facilitate reconnecting with the self . . . and with something larger than the self
- To create opportunity for articulating and reflecting on the meaning of personal connections
- To promote appreciation for life as it is right now
- [If used in a group setting] To provide a safer, more ideal way of having members introduce themselves.

When something difficult happens, and we don't have people around to provide support, help, context, care, or attunement, we can easily feel isolated, alienated, or lonely. To counter that, it's important to acknowledge and welcome whatever is causing the discomfort while also cultivating ground for connection—to recognize what we belong to.

Many of us who have had painful histories feel we don't belong to other people, a specific group or culture, or even this earth . . . let alone ourselves. Yet we still long for more, for better, for what often feels elusive. That longing to belong can point us in the direction we want to go, toward the possibility of being connected and essential in the scheme of life. If we look beyond our fears or habitual thought patterns, we may even find we are already connected in a myriad of ways.

When we remind ourselves that we already *do* belong, it gives us the opportunity to explore what we *want* to belong to. For people who have histories of pain, it can seem as though they belong to the pain—to the past. We need to remember that we don't have to belong to our pain or only identify with that part of our history.

Instead we can wonder: What would it take to belong to the people, places, and things in our lives that offer us kindness, nurturance, and joy?

One of the challenges facing trauma survivors is balancing the yearning of wanting to feel safe and loved against the protective impulse to isolate that accompanies that longing. Learning to distinguish where that impulse to isolate is coming from is important. Learning to be conscious of these two states allows us the ability to choose engagement when we feel ready, but also honors the need for quiet time.

During a conversation I had with poet David Whyte, my eyes were opened to the importance of belonging. I was describing to him the work I do with trauma survivors and it inevitably led to a conversation about the suffering they live with. He brought up the intrinsic need of *belonging*. I wondered aloud about belongingness with respect to the people I worked with, as they often don't think they belong anywhere.

David pointed out that they do belong; everyone belongs somewhere. He reflected that some of my clients might feel they belong to the hospitals they'd been in, or perhaps they identified with the suffering they had endured. He suggested that I find a way to orient them to other—less traumatic—forms of belonging.

In the BSE online groups and courses, people have realized that connections can be formed through recollecting cherished memories and holding on to keepsakes. Developing an expanded sense of self and connecting to other participants in the online group, members of their families, or with their cultures and the planet are important aspects in creating a healthy notion of belonging.

Feeling connected to something larger than the mundane—some greater reality or presence that's larger than the trauma—can also remind us of what helps us feel safe. In fact, many may feel abandoned by life, God, or by any good and nourishing things. Encouraging a sense of belongingness helps individuals to reconnect not only to themselves but to the larger world.

For people who have known a lot of pain it can be complicated looking for other ways to connect. Learning about the many places we belong that aren't just about the pain we're in gives us a way to get to know each other. Having an emphasis on belonging is a way to have stories building on connection, kindness, and joy.

If you're someone who has difficulty talking about yourself (which many people do), this can give you a safer way to express yourself. Knowing yourself in ways that go beyond the painful moments you've had can give you a way to be present to yourself in an embodied way. For many, sharing or journaling meaningful stories allows them to appreciate and remember the gifts they've been given.

Sharing stories also provides a norm about communicating, building a space of appreciation, encouraging a caring attitude, and generating interest in oneself and in others.

Invite yourself and encourage others to share what is important. Join around the connection, experiencing the empathy and understanding which helps develop a larger connection to people, places, or events.

This process of finding connection through belonging generates a way of connecting on many levels, both to what's meaningful to you, as well as hearing what's meaningful for others.

You'll discover how meaning arises through these connections, and how people feel valued for the small, simple gifts of who they are and what they can contribute to the world—all of which helps point you in the direction you want to go in this life.

The exercise begins with finding objects, words, phrases, or pictures that echo the unique way that life and history have shaped you and helped you to feel connected, to people, places, events, situations, and objects. It's been a gift for me when people bring in photos of those people and pets they love, places they feel alive, stones from specific places, or objects that others have given to them. The stories are rich and vibrant with meaning.

One woman brought in a sprig of fresh rosemary; it reminded her of her grandmother's garden, which she considered a safe harbor. Another woman brought in shells that magically appeared at the foot of her beach house one night when she felt called to go outside at 2 a.m. Whether mundane or deeply moving, their stories come alive. I, we, are invited into their world.

The next step could be to reflect on how your life—both the joy and the suffering—is a gift, and how those gifts can suggest certain life directions once you've appreciated their meaning.

And, I will suggest a way for you to make the skill portable, so you have it when you need it in your daily life!

Suzanne shared, "I think I was struggling to define what belongingness was and struggling to find a warm connected experience, because I struggle to find safe comfortable feelings. I had a part of me convinced that I had no belonging."

Suzanne gives us a powerful example that speaks to belonging. A part of Suzanne felt ostracized. Doing this exercise is a way to observe, know, and heal these various aspects of ourselves. Her felt experience was saying, "I want to have a safe comfortable feeling, but because I don't have a safe comfortable feeling, I don't belong."

EXERCISE: CHERISHED OBJECTS, MEMORIES, AND CONNECTIONS

This is a wonderful time to look for an object (or objects) that represents something that gives you a sense of belonging. This is a time to explore, to be curious, to wonder about what connection is for you. What brings it about? How has it occurred in the past?

This can be a way for you to engage with others, using the object as a way to share what's meaningful for you. As I said, over the time I've done this with others, people have brought in pictures of loved ones; something from a holiday celebration; a poem; a seashell from a favorite vacation—things that symbolize memories of good feelings, safety, or love. Connecting to people as they share these stories contributes to a larger tapestry of connection that we can draw on when things get tough.

Of course, it goes without saying that it is essential to feel free NOT to share. I am constantly reminding people that, "There is NO right or wrong way to do this exercise or anything else I suggest."

If this isn't the right time to do this exercise, trust it. Let the protest emerge and wonder what need it's trying to orient you toward. Each exercise I suggest is designed as an invitation to explore your inner world. Only you know what's right for you at any one time.

Another Suggestion: A Belonging Box

In this version of the exercise (or as a second part to the one above), you can gather words, quotes, sentences, pictures, or memorabilia to put in a small box, perhaps only the size of a breath mint tin. Ideally, the box should be easily portable and always available. You could also make a collage or mini scrapbook that fits into a daily planner so it's readily at hand. Pinterest is a good place to do this as well, though be sure you're clear on what's private and what is shared.

Either way, over time, collect items that speak to you of your connections to the past, present, and/or future. Welcome your creativity. If you have a special little basket or bag, use that. In addition to the small wonders around your home and yard, be on the lookout for little natural wonders or trinkets that speak to you of connection. Once you've established a mini-collection, you can always pull something from your box to help you talk about experiences, or simply remind yourself of times that feel meaningful, things that represent good feelings, vibration, love, joy, happiness, and contentment.

Here's one of the key things we can all try: When we're in those states, when we are in a place of "I'm not enough, my life is not enough, or good things aren't happening" we'll have thoughts like: nobody loves me, I don't belong here, or no one understands me.

However, what we can do is find or access a time when we felt a warm connected experience. It's akin to being engrossed in a book or a movie, so you have that experience to guide yourself. You know what I mean? The research term for that emotional processing is called simulated experience. We can simulate our internal world by imagining something so then our body has an experience, but our body cannot distinguish whether this simulated experience is something "real" or in the present. Enough research has been done on mirror and motor neurons to know that our felt experience from memory has the same effect on our body as an experience that we're actually feeling in the moment. Let's say you're playing with a puppy or you see a child at the grocery store. The puppy and child are just playing and being silly; they're alive. Just hang out with that experience and stay with it for as long as you can. The more we hang onto any experience, whether it's for a few seconds, seventeen seconds, or thirty seconds, our brain starts shifting, priming itself to move in a new way.

This is a good thing to try when you're feeling less triggered. It's easier to practice, to be curious, to be open to new learning when our bodies are balanced. When we're triggered it's a much harder concept to put into practice. Yet, the more we practice the feeling of having a warm connected experience, the more our body will naturally move in that direction, and the more easily that connected experience will happen in our life.

BELONGING

Take a moment to jot down a few thoughts in response to the following questions.

If you feel desperate to belong, what do you tend to grab on to? Is it a specific person, a familiar place, or something else like food, sex, working out, self-destructive behaviors, isolating, fantasizing?

_____

_____

_____

_____

_____

_____

Are there other people, places, situations, activities, concepts, or feelings that you would rather belong to? What are they?

_____

_____

_____

_____

_____

_____

Where in your body do you feel a sense of connectedness/belonging? And where do you feel or notice a feeling of disconnection?

_____

_____

_____

_____

_____

_____

How does your body communicate that information to you? Let go of old meanings and associations that you have unconsciously learned that may cluster around various areas of your body. When you drop or stop focusing on those stories, what does your body tell you? What sensations do you feel right now?

_____

_____

_____

_____

_____

_____

SKILL 2: MEDITATION

Mindfulness

Objectives:
- To develop an observing sense of self that is more inclusive and stable
- To strengthen our capacity to watch, observe, and note without getting caught up in what is being observed
- To increase our ability to distinguish and name previously unnamable thoughts/feelings
- To support dis-identifying with whatever happens to be arising within
- To learn to befriend symptoms, feelings, and parts of us that feel over-whelming
- To relax and be at rest

Over the years, I've had trauma survivors ask me what skills would help them most. I tell them, "Three things: You need to be able to focus on where you want to go, witness what you're going through without getting overwhelmed, and practice self-compassion."

In this module, I introduce the two main forms of meditation. One form emphasizes focus and concentration while the second form centers on mindfulness (the most common meditation practice in the West). Mindfulness develops the capacity to notice and observe what's happening without getting too hooked on any one observation.

However, it's essential that we learn and develop self-compassion, to welcome negative self-talk, as we gain more experience meditating. Self-compassion is an overarching theme binding the modules of this course together.

Meditation "involves making our mind familiar with positive states such as love, compassion, patience, serenity, and wisdom, so that these become more natural and spontaneous. Then, when we encounter an unkind or hostile person, we'll be more likely to remain calm and patient, and even feel compassion for them" (Kathleen McDonald, *How to Meditate*, (2005).

With practice, meditation can help us in varied ways: to put aside the distractions of daily life, to slow down and become more aware of our inner states, to cultivate a sense of inner calm, and to feel renewed. But that's all much easier said than done, especially for trauma survivors, who often experience their inner world as frantic, chaotic, and overwhelming. Most long for a way to become calm inside, but can't imagine how to do it. They're constantly engaged in negative self-talk and worn thin by vitriolic inner chatter.

Over the years, I have learned how to guide trauma survivors to experience a quiet state in meditation that is contained, resourceful, and replenishing. With time and practice, they begin to accumulate moments of quiet that help to calm their nervous systems and invite a connection to the sacred.

Developing a meditation practice needs to be done carefully and gradually, as too many unwelcome emotions can come up too fast for trauma survivors to handle. Meditation practice may also incline certain clients to enter a regressive state (i.e., when a vulnerable or triggered state causes you to temporarily regress to an earlier stage or moment in your life).

Mindfulness and Concentration

Mindfulness practices ask us to notice and name whatever is occurring . . . and then gently let those observations go. They develop the aspect of our consciousness that can fluidly observe our inner selves without getting stuck on any one observation.

Concentration practices ask us to focus our attention on one thing to the exclusion of all else. Both skills—observing and focusing—are essential for healing trauma. Observing allows clients to be in touch with all parts of being, thereby encouraging integration; focusing helps them direct their attention to where they want to go—away from the pull of triggers.

Self-compassion is generally a concentration practice, in that it focuses the mind. Because it's so essential to healing, I'm adding it here as a separate component.

Mindfulness Practices

Mindfulness meditation can put us into more direct contact with our inner states by helping us quiet the internal chatter, so we can begin to see the previously imperceptible components of each thought, feeling, sensation, and impulse.

We are always giving our attention to something, either the present moment (which would be mindfulness) or to the past, which consists of the habitual, automatic thoughts of our minds.

When we're in the here and now, we're accepting everything without judgment or reaction. We tend to be in more of an inclusive and loving state of mind. One way to practice mindfulness might be to find ways to sustain appropriate attention throughout the day.

Thich Nhat Hanh, a monk from Vietnam, writes that we experience miracles when we practice mindfulness. Examples of such miracles include being able to deeply touch the blue sky, a flower, or the smile of a child. When we really "see" these things or take them in, we feel real—alive. When we're not present in this way, he says, everything feels like a dream.

Once we are present and mindful, we can nourish the object of our attention. Our attention will "water the wilting flower." This kind of attention—this mindfulness—truly eases our suffering. When we're not present, we can't relieve any suffering. When we are mindful, we see, know, and are present to that which is, which includes both joy and suffering, without passing judgment on either state.

The Sanskrit word for mindfulness is *smriti,* which means, "to remember." In this sense, mindfulness is remembering to come back to the present moment with all its love, pain, terror, softness, and kindness.

Mindfulness meditation helps to make room for choice by opening the space between impulse and action, between feeling and doing.

Developing mindfulness skills increases a person's chances of using other Becoming Safely Embodied skills, such as:

- "Noting" (an essential component of mindfulness that allows facts to be separated from feelings/interpretations), which allows us to slow down our minds more easily—to notice what is happening inside ourselves and to engage our frontal lobes. [See Skill 6: "Suggestions for Developing Wholesome Self-talk: 1. Dis-Identifying" for more about Noting]
- Parallel Lives (which will be introduced in BSE Skill 5) are then more easily deconstructed.
- Soothing dysregulated parts is easier if we can notice and dis-identify from them.

As we become aware and note what is happening inside ourselves, we begin to discern and undermine the habitual internal dialogues we are constantly having with ourselves. Mindfulness meditation puts us into direct contact with what we might call our "True Self" or "Authentic Self." Some people call it an "Abiding Self." Contacting ourselves through mindfulness meditation happens by doing the following:

Slowing Down Internal Chatter

What begins to happen, especially as you practice these skills, is you'll find you can observe what is going on in slower motion. It's like you begin to see life frame by frame. You'll train yourself to see the imperceptible building blocks of each thought/feeling/impulse.

Providing Choice

Mindfulness opens an opportunity for clarity in our experience, a gap between impulse and action, so that you can choose a healthier avenue to take. It also helps us develop our understanding of what's going on. Understanding in that way is a key component of wisdom. Knowing how something works allows us to free ourselves from its dominance.

Mindfulness Practice Suggestions

Find a quiet space wherever you are and become comfortable. Notice your body relaxing. The simple act of *noticing* already orients you toward mindfulness.

Let yourself become aware of whatever is there. Simply notice it. You will become aware of being pulled in one direction or another. Perhaps you'll feel inclined toward getting more involved with what you are observing, or you may be repelled by what you are observing. You might go blank. Just notice whatever happens.

The second most helpful skill to practice in mindfulness is to simply label whatever it is you are observing. If a previous conversation arises, take note and label it, "talking." Breathe and relax; notice "talking." The old story will probably not immediately disappear, especially if you are accustomed to thinking about it, or if the subject has a heavy emotional charge. In that case, just keep naming and labeling. Remember that ingrained habits and self-talk take time to change.

If you are unable to shift out of the intensity of the subject, you may want to try some form of concentration practice (such as *metta*) to have your mind focus on something else.

Mindfulness Meditation for Trauma Survivors

Benefits of Mindfulness Meditation
- Builds an observing self that counteracts the inner critic
- Acts as an uncovering technique that reveals unexamined aspects of yourself
- Allows you to identify and name previously unnamable thoughts/feelings
- Decreases identification with what's happening, allowing you to simply be there with yourself

31

- Moves you from a sense of chronic vulnerability to one of greater equilibrium
- Generates relaxation—a feeling of being at rest

Cautions of Mindfulness Meditation
- Not everyone is ready to use an uncovering technique. Too much may come up too quickly.
- If too much comes up at once, it can bring on regressive states

General Suggestions for Practice
When I first started teaching meditation to trauma survivors in the 1990s it became clear that taking in a moment of ease through meditation made it easier to attempt another time. If the first couple of experiences are good, then it's easier to have the next couple.

It's so important to try meditating at a pace that works for you. Many people find they need to start with a very short period at first, perhaps one to three minutes, noticing what happens without judging or criticizing yourself. If the first practice is a helpful experience, you can practice again, either later in the day or the next day. The more comfortable it is, the easier it is to practice—being with yourself, watching what floats through your inner world. We think one minute is so little, but when we sit with ourselves, that one minute can be very full!

If the experience was not very helpful or restful, and you're okay trying again, it might be good to wait until the next day. If you're reluctant, that's not a problem.

If meditating by yourself is difficult, try recalling how you were feeling when you tried to practice. Were you calm? Agitated? Nervous? Watchful? Were you regressed or in a younger self-state? As you explore, identify, and describe what happened, it can be helpful to journal as a way to get to know yourself in this new way.

Anyone who tries to develop a new practice or habit knows how difficult it can be to set up and maintain. Helpful suggestions to support your practice include:
- Consider if you'd find it easier to practice in the morning or evening.
- Limit distractions by turning off phones, putting your pet in another room, etc.
- Read something inspirational before starting meditation.
- Feeling anxious or agitated? Go for a short walk or stretch before beginning.
- In whatever position you sit, you need to make sure your body is reasonably relaxed.

Josephine: My intention is to find balance and start small. This focus on the breath was the perfect gift to support the intention. The breath is simple, yet so rich and meaningful. Deirdre always reminds me there are two journeys. The first is to go from outside to inside. Then to drop out of my head and into my heart. I noticed that moving from external to internal was subtly calming. I felt my shoulders soften slightly and the muscles in my face eased a bit. My awareness of my body breathing increased almost instantly. The attention on the nano-movements of the in breath and the out breath was cool. I noticed so much . . . then the thoughts crept in and the awareness of my body faded. I reconnected with Deirdre's calming voice and brought my focus back to my breath. I felt the breath movements again and noticed a new tightness and a disappointment—or a longing for the ease I had felt just moments earlier, which pulled me back into thoughts. The gentleness of recorded voice and the invitation back to the breath eased me back. Through this brief practice, I recognized the wisdom of the intention to start small.

I invite you to access additional free online book bonuses: dfay.com/resources

EXERCISE: MINDFULNESS MEDITATION

1. Remind yourself you only need to practice only for a short time in the beginning, starting with a few seconds, progressing to one to three minutes.
2. The first step is to find a quiet space and become comfortable. Many people close their eyes to meditate, while others find that a soft, open unfocused gaze works better for them.
3. Notice your breathing, paying attention to what it's like to shift your attention from outside to inside. The simple act of *noticing* already orients you toward mindfulness. The soft breath can be grounding. It also serves as the main object of attention to return to whenever the mind drifts. The practice revolves around noticing the breath and returning one's attention to breathing when distractions arise.
4. Simply notice whatever is happening when seated. Often attention might get more involved with what you are thinking, observing, feeling, judging, or your mind may go blank. The key is to notice whatever happens without judgment and avoid trying to fix it. If you go blank, can you explore the blankness? How

big is it? What color or shape? Are there any sounds associated with the blankness? Try to engage around it as much as you can.

5. "Labeling" is another helpful technique to practice along with mindful observation. Use a word or phrase to label whatever you are observing. If a previous conversation arises in your head, notice it and label it as "talking" or "remembering," after which steer your attention back to breathing. In this process, you are training yourself to keep your attention on the act of (and increasing your capacity for) noticing, rather than focusing on the content of what you are noticing, or the emotional charge that the content contains.

6. Reassure yourself that most of us can only hold our attention for seconds at a time. Our minds tend to drift. The intention in practicing meditation is not to do it flawlessly. It's more important to self-compassionately notice that our minds have drifted and to refocus on the object of our attention (breath).

There are definitely times when we can get stuck in repeating old tapes, or caught in intense emotions or sensations; that's a good time to shift to a concentration practice such as *metta*, or with your eyes open to focus on a noise, color, or image.

If it was a helpful experience, then practice again either later in the day or the next day. If you feel comfortable with it, increase your time a minute or two when you feel right about it. If the experience was not helpful or restful, and you feel comfortable trying again, wait until the next day.

If you don't want to try again, no problem. You may find concentration practices work better for you.

Take a mental scan of the state you were in when you tried to practice. Were you calm? Agitated? Nervous? Watchful? Were you in a younger feeling-state?

Anyone who undertakes a spiritual practice knows how difficult it can be to set one up. Take stock of what worked, and what you want to have different next time.

- Did the time of day work for you?
- Were there any distractions? Is there something you can do differently next time?
- Did it help to read something inspirational before you start?
- What state was your body in before, during, and after? Is there something you would do differently next time to make it easier? If your body is agitated, go for a short walk, or stretch your muscles before you begin.

EXERCISE: RESTING IN THE BREATH

First practice resting in the breath, which means doing nothing other than focusing your attention on the breath at either the tip of the nostril, or as the breath fills your lungs/belly. This does not mean holding your breath, it is simply a gentle focus on a specific place in the body where the breath engages naturally. Try letting the breath "hold" you, just as your body or the chair is holding you. If your internal world feels too overwhelming, practice naming or noting, whatever is coming up (ex. "feelings, feelings" or "thinking, thinking." Or "planning, planning.") By simply labeling what is churning up inside ourselves, and gently refocusing on our breath, you can externalize, or dis-identify, from the material. This begins the process of witnessing what's happening, instead of being pulled into it.

EXERCISE: NOTICING WITH BARE ATTENTION

For this experience, find a location and define the geographical area that you intend to pay attention to. It might be a wall, the space between a desk and a door, or the space between one house and another. Then notice what is there. Take the time to name things without commentary or judgment, and to then let the names drift away like passing clouds.

To help with this you could make a list of what you see, or draw whatever you observe, refraining from embellishment. Instead of writing a story about what you're seeing, this is a time to make simple observations about color, texture, shape, and object name (e.g. white desk, cracked sidewalk, dim table lamp, jagged piece of glass). Keep your observations as simple and uncomplicated as possible.

Our minds are prone toward complexity and association (e.g. that awful old white desk, my mother gave me that, or that dangerous piece of jagged glass, etc.). It's easy to get caught in those story lines. The practice, here, is to 1) let whatever is there rise into awareness, 2) note it, and 3) let it pass away.

Another option is to listen attentively to some music. Here again, notice the impulse to assign meaning or associate with what you hear. Welcome that impulse, but turn your attention to simply listen and notice the elements (e.g. the sounds, rhythms, volume, and tempo). What happens as you become aware of the silence between the notes, as well as the notes arising in patterns from the silence. Of course, your mind may wander (as all of ours do!) and need to be coaxed gently back to bare noticing.

If you have a trusted friend, it can be a good experience to do together. You'll most likely find that your friend sees and hears different things from you. It makes for a perfect conversation about how people see things differently AND how various parts within us can see the same thing through different windows of experience too.

Practicing Mindfulness On Your Own

This is a practice . . . watching and naming what goes on inside ourselves, creating room. In that process we clear inner ground, allowing ourselves to be delighted when a moment of clarity and calm happens.

What keeps those moments from happening? You might find, as so many of us do, that we start to judge and negatively evaluate what is happening, leaving this *here and now moment* and going to the *past*. These past moments, which I call "time capsules" (see Skill 5: Addressing Parallel Lives) are full of thoughts, feelings, sensations, memories, and impulses. These time capsules are full of good times and the many times when we learned to feel bad, wrong, or shamed. The result is that now we become afraid, negative, and/or judgmental whenever we are confronted by similar or related experiences. Practicing staying in the here and now helps to keep us grounded and oriented toward where we want to go.

MINDFULNESS PRACTICES REFLECTION

Take a moment to jot down a few thoughts in response to the following questions.

Try to notice, with bare attention, when you find you're treating yourself harshly, such as criticizing or judging yourself. Some people find it helpful to keep a list of instances when they default to old, destructive behaviors. Reducing the frequency of these negative behaviors indicates that you are making progress.

_____
_____
_____
_____
_____

What was the "here and now" situation/context in which the harsh self-talk occurred?

_____
_____

_____
_____
_____

Is there anything familiar in what happened? What's familiar may reside within a tone of voice, a gesture, or a feeling that comes up inside of you. What "there-and-then" moments are the familiar experiences anchored in? Just notice. Practice non-judgmental observing as much as you can.[1]

_____
_____
_____
_____
_____

Concentration

Objectives:

- To counterbalance negative messages and self-images
- To focus the mind and calm the self
- To learn how to effectively shift attention toward positive states
- To feel less like victims of negative self-states
- To tolerate and promote good feelings

Concentration practices encourage the mind to grow in the direction you want it to—away from those areas you don't want it to grow." (Gehlek Rimpoche) Those who have suffered from trauma know how hard it can be to focus the mind or stay directed without losing course. Frequently, we get derailed by the noise or chaos going on inside. Perhaps we have a lot of feelings coming up at once, or overwhelming feelings; we might be caught in ruminations, revenge fantasies, or even several competing conversations about what's right or wrong. Or numbness.

Research indicates that our minds only stay on one thing for three to seven seconds before we skip to the next thing. Advertising and media have learned how

---

1   Optional Reading: *Practicing Mindfulness in Sacred Practices* by Nancy Napier and *How to Meditate* by Kathleen McDonald.

to engage our minds by constantly shifting images. If, however, we are overloaded with upsetting internal stimuli, it's a good practice to learn to keep our minds steady.

One of the key skills we can learn is how to concentrate and focus. Imagine how useful focusing the mind might be upon being emotionally triggered. Almost immediately, we're overtaken by the urge to head down a swirling path, usually with protective parts wanting to find a way to calm the situation down. The triggered tsunami threatens to overtake us. In order to know why this happened, it's important to slow down the triggered tsunami. This is a great benefit of concentration practices. We narrow our field of focus, which allows everything else to fade back. Any kind of concentration practice can help with that. It can be as simple as practicing multiplication tables. Or singing.

One of the concentration practices that people have used in the BSE groups is cultivating loving kindness. It's one of four practices that support building the Brahma-viharas or what is translated as "the heavenly abodes of the mind." These abodes include *metta* (loving kindness), *karuna* (compassion), *upeka (*equanimity), and *mudita (*joyful appreciation).

I've found *metta* to be an antidote to the negative messages that people tell themselves or have heard repeatedly from others. Practicing *metta* (loving kindness) is one way to slowly discharge the negativity from those messages that reinforce a crippling self-image. It's a practice that can develop our capacity to focus attention on what you want—directing your energy as a way to cultivate positive regard and feelings of loving kindness toward ourselves, and contributing to the making of a kinder world.

The classic way to practice *metta* is to silently recite and repeat four phrases, savoring each phrase before going on to the next. Sharon Salzberg is the Buddhist teacher who popularized this practice in the West. Her beautiful book *Loving Kindness: The Revolutionary Art of Happiness*, is a wonderful reference if you are looking for more information on *metta*.

These are the traditional four phrases of *metta:*
May I be happy.
May I be at peace.
May I live with ease.
May I be free from suffering.
Some people find that these phrases aren't quite a fit for them. They might choose to recite different phrases—a mantra, a simple centering prayer, a few nurturing affirmations of their own choosing, or a structured prayer with prayer beads.

The most important thing is to choose a phrase(s) or word(s) that allows you to focus without getting entangled in the associations to the word. If the phrase, "May

I be happy" brings up too much commentary from the internal "peanut gallery" (for example, parts of you might be quite vocal about why they should never, ever be happy!) then it's going to be too disturbing to sit with. That won't help to build a sense of quiet inside!

If you prefer use phrases from other spiritual traditions or make up your own phrases. Some people have chosen phrases like, "May I be happy someday," "May I be calm," "May I be gentler with myself," or "May I be free from self-harm."

Ideally, the phrases will become a beacon for your mind, without becoming objectionable or something you'll resist. Most importantly, it encourages a state of mind which is conducive to mental ease, without kicking up too much dust.

As Kathleen McDonald (2005) writes in her classic book, *How to Meditate*, "Don't worry if you don't actually feel love; it's enough to say these words and think these thoughts. In time, the feeling will come." We're encouraging the formation of new neural connections by repeating these words and intending their outcome.

At some point, the feelings start aligning with that intention. It's a helpful exercise for anyone who tends to feel that their feelings of hardship and pain are "the only way it can be." As you learn to be open to all your feelings with self-compassion, you can *choose* the feelings you want, which leads to a wonderful sense of empowerment. It's out of this that a sense of agency develops, leading to confidence in one's self.

Without exaggeration, *metta* and other concentration practices can be one of the most powerful skills that trauma survivors can learn. When hijacked by the limbic system—or overwhelmed with obsessive thinking, anxiety, depression, or flashbacks—trauma survivors can, with practice, learn to shift their self-state by using concentration practices.

Metta practices should, at the same time, be adopted with care. They can engender a state of bliss that may be scary for those with trauma histories. Saying anything even remotely positive can generate intense self-hatred. The parts of the psyche that object to feeling good can assert themselves. In a blissful state, boundaries may be experienced as too diffuse, leaving us feeling unsafe or out of control. It can also trigger regression. In some people, particularly those who have difficulty tolerating positive-affect states, a *metta* practice may initially prompt an oppositional reaction, intensifying self-hatred.

If it's too hard to say *metta* for yourself it may be helpful, or easier, to say *metta* for someone else, a much-loved relative, your pet, or even a neutral person such as the person at the pharmacy counter or someone you're walking past on the street.

Some clients find value in offering *metta* to the parts of themselves that are suffering, annoyed, angry, or sad.

Working with negative reactions to the practice involves balancing the negative with the positive. For example, you can name the self-talk that is there, "I hate myself," by balancing it with "and I wish to be at peace;" or offset "I'm such a loser" with "and I want to be free of that painful perspective." We need to remind ourselves that we are free to always choose the antidote—bringing in the "and" statement, rather than staying stuck with only the negative.

One year I was heading to a long-term meditation retreat when I stopped in New York City to visit a friend. I left my suitcases in the back of my car, filled with the clothes and books I was bringing on retreat. When I came out from the visit, I was horrified to see my car broken in and all my things gone. Somehow, I got to the retreat. Once there, I laid in my bed shaking, letting the trauma move through my body. During the many days that followed I would say, "My body is shaking . . . and may I be at peace." And, "This was horrible . . . and may I live with ease."

Adding the simple word "and" allowed me to validate my experience while offering myself the blessing, orienting me to where I wanted to go.

There might be times when you might find sitting meditation difficult. This is where *metta* can be such a good resource. It's ideal when going for a walk, helping you to move stuck energy and as an important way to focus.

Other helpful tools are to practice dis-identifying from the self-hatred by switching to mindfulness meditation, or focus your attention on something tangible in the physical world, using mindfulness to note objects in the room (door, lamp, clock, magazine, etc.). You can also choose a different activity such as reading, working out, watching TV, cleaning, or doing something soothing and re-regulating. One of the checklists I use in the BSE online course, "Being Different with Triggers," can help when you're triggered. Use this link to access it for free: dfay.com/resources

Here are some guidelines before you start *metta***:**

To do the *metta* exercise, you'll need three or four benevolent phrases that invite a positive internal experience. As I mentioned, the traditional *metta* phrases are:

- May I be happy.
- May I be at peace.
- May I live with ease.
- May I be free from suffering.

Do those suit you? Is there something else you would prefer? It might be a phrase, a mantra, a chorus from a song, a repetitive movement, a simple centering prayer, a few nurturing affirmations of your own, or a structured prayer with (or without) prayer beads.

You could also shift to mindfulness practice and note whatever is arising from within. Mindfulness practice often creates space between how you see yourself in the moment and the thoughts or feelings that are coming up.

Benefits of a Concentration Practice:
- Focusing creates the opportunity for calm and even blissful states.
- Concentration trains the mind to focus, rather than be scattered.
- The ability to direct your experience is strengthened.
- You begin to recognize that you're not at the mercy of your mind-states.

Cautions of a Concentration Practice:
- Since internal boundaries are relaxed, there may be a tendency to feel out of control. It can be hard to know where you begin and end.
- Regression becomes more probable.
- Self-hate can initially intensify.

EXERCISE: METTA

Find a quiet space and sit comfortably; or try while walking. Take a few long breaths. What would help you relax just a little bit more? Softly focus your eyes on a spot in front of you or close your eyes if that is more comfortable.

Find a phrase(s) that feels nurturing and satisfying for you—something that you want to cultivate. Begin saying that phrase, or several phrases to yourself. Say the first. Let that settle in. Then say the next (or repeat the first). Again, breathe in and let that settle in before moving on to the next.

Be as repetitive as you want, for as long as you like. Allow yourself to resonate with these qualities.

Don't be concerned if you find yourself resonating with the opposite of the phrase (for example, if you're feeling angry instead of happy). If that happens, just let go of the practice and come back to it again for a shorter period. Start with one to five minutes and as it becomes more comfortable, add a little more time.

Remember, there is no right way to do this. It's a practice to find the softest, easiest, most comfortable way to develop concentration. Don't push yourself if it doesn't feel right. Just try it again another time. If you notice that you're berating yourself, for whatever reason, practice self-compassion. And focus on your desire to feel good (another kind of concentration practice) instead of feeling bad.

Variations:

- Focus your attention on feelings of love, wellbeing, or kindness. Notice where that energy lives in your body and what that feels like in your body. You may even hear yourself say things such as, "This feels good," or "Gosh, this is restful." Whatever you notice, smile and take it in. It's akin to saturating your body, mind, and heart in heartwarming energy. Take some time to breathe that positive energy in and out. Let it be like a fountain that flows up from inside you, spilling over and throughout your body. Breathe in the energy, revel in it, then exhale.

- Practice sending *metta* to your body, an individual part, or a cluster of parts. In traditional practice you first would begin sending *metta* to yourself, then someone neutral, then a difficult person, continuing to expand into the universe until you have saturated the energetic universe with loving-kindness.

- One of my practices as a therapist is to take a moment in between sessions to send *metta* to myself—and to my client. I find taking that moment can be more refreshing than drinking a cup of coffee!

EXERCISE: OFFERING AND RECEIVING BLESSINGS

Materials needed: paper, pens, pencils, crayons, colored pencils.

Most everyone has received gifts for holidays and birthdays. This can provoke a variety of feelings. Learning to give and receive is important in remapping our inner world, away from the old and toward a more beneficent one. It's a meditation combined with an art project. Remind yourself that gifts can be non-physical.

Begin by quieting yourself, transitioning your attention from the external world to your internal experience. If it feels right, close your eyes.

Remember instances when you offered and received gifts.

Go through the following questions, reflecting in quiet, writing your responses in your journal:

- Were these happy times?
- Did you feel burdened by having to give a gift?
- Was it difficult for you to try to find the right present?
- What reactions did you expect when you gave someone a gift?

42

- What messages did you want to receive?
- What is it that you dearly longed for, yet believed would never happen?
- What would you like to offer others?
- What is it like to receive?
- What thoughts come up that prevent you from receiving?

Afterwards, create a greeting card that expresses a blessing you would want to give or receive. This certainly doesn't have to be fabulous, "finished," or elegant. It's a time to explore, to wonder, to be open.

Imagine giving someone you care about this blessing. How do you imagine they'll receive it? Focus on how you imagine they'll receive the spirit of the blessing, less so the card itself. Is there someone you feel safe actually giving the blessing to? What is the expression you would like to receive in kind?

Practicing this experience is a way for us to introduce ourselves, especially parts of us that we ordinarily hold back. It's not unusual for people to be afraid to do the exercise. If you have the courage to share the blessing with someone, notice how they respond. If they don't respond in the way you would have wished, can you welcome in that unmet need as information about what's important to you?

CONCENTRATION PRACTICES: METTA (LOVING-KINDNESS) REFLECTION

Take a moment to jot down a few thoughts in response to the following questions.

> "That I feed the beggar, that I forgive an insult, that I love my enemy … all these are undoubtedly great virtues … But what if I should discover that the least among them all, the poorest of the beggars, the most impudent of all offenders, yea the very fiend himself—that these are within me, and that I myself stand in the need of the alms of my own kindness, that I myself am the enemy who must be loved—what then?"
> —Carl Jung, *Psychology and Religion: West and East*

Notice how often you feel you need to give to others instead of yourself. What would it be like at those times to stop and observe the thoughts, feelings, and impulses that arise when you don't automatically act? It may be hard to do, but give it a try.

What are your familiar behaviors? What's familiar about them? How do you usually feel after doing the "normal" behaviors?

_____
_____
_____
_____
_____
_____

Are there thoughts and feelings about *not* engaging in this same behavior? What do you imagine will happen if you don't do this?

_____
_____
_____
_____
_____
_____

What happens if you give to yourself that which you want to give to another?

_____
_____
_____
_____
_____
_____

Explore this approach with yourself. Have fun! There's no "right" way to do any of this.[2]

Self-Compassion and Attachment in Healing Shame

Objectives:
- Counteract self-criticism, self-blame, self-judgment

---

2 **Optional Reading:** Chapter 2, *Relearning Loveliness in Loving Kindness: The Revolutionary Art of Happiness* by Sharon Salzberg

- Promote a growth-oriented attitude and support ability to change
- Reduce suffering by creating a balance of warmth
- Cultivate seeing the best in ourselves and in others
- Develop our common humanity, recognizing we all suffer
- Offer protection against anxiety and depression

Attachment and Self-Compassion

Reading the research on attachment theory and watching children, it occurred to me that something fundamental is happening. There's an attachment cycle we all live in. We have a comfort zone we each inhabit. Becoming more secure in life is to widen that comfort zone so we're more and more comfortable in a variety of places, situations, and other people. That comfort zone is what John Bowlby called the "secure base." It's where we feel safe, settled, and comfortable.

In an ideal situation, when a child has older, wiser people attuning to her as she develops, curious about who she is inside, how she's similar and also fascinated with how different she is, something wonderful happens—this child begins to develop this inner sense of self. This entranced state of infant and caregiver creates a fused world, captivated by each other.

Have you had that experience? Of being with an infant, watching every breath, captivated by the movement of the fingers. In an ideal world, this important time of fusion creates a bubble in which the infant experiences physical safety and emotional attunement.

Held in the comforting container of the safety of others, she organically, almost through osmosis, learns to harness, contain, and structure the energy of life pouring through her nervous system. As this child learns how to flow with this inner state, a sense of self develops; contained within appropriate boundaries this child naturally expresses her wants, wishes, and needs—expecting those needs to be met.

Over time, this inner secure base facilitates the infant expressing not just vocally but also through movement. Contained in safety the infant shifts and moves and stretches the boundary of what is known, exploring the world outside by crawling, reaching, grabbing, tasting. Without concepts of what's good or bad, right or wrong, the infant becomes a toddler, transforming into a child who loves to express, courageously stepping outside the known world, experimenting, all while knowing there are safe people to turn to, who will provide reassurance and comfort when the inevitable turbulence comes when stretching outside the comfort zone.

To grossly oversimplify our world, we have two competing systems battling for our attention. The one we're so familiar with is the fear that urges us to keep safe, to stay within the known. And yet there's this second internal system that drives us to explore, to reach beyond.

These two primary systems are hardwired. The need to belong and be emotionally connected joins with our need for physical security. As human beings we need to know we belong, that we're securely connected, wanted just as we are. When we feel safely connected, our body naturally calms with a reassuring sense that everything will be okay. Loneliness eases as we rely on others who are at the same time respecting our internal knowing of what to do, where to go, who we are.

Without these support systems built into our everyday world growing up, we are more prone to negative self-talk, catastrophizing, fearful of the next crushing blow of life. Without this inner secure base, Jeremy Holmes, the attachment theorist, wrote in 2001 " . . . minor setbacks may come to look like disasters; the world becomes threatening; the mental pain associated with loss of status, rather than acting as a spur to the formation of new bonds, may gain a life of its own and feel overwhelming." (Holmes, 2001, p. 2)

Attachment theory describes not only physical safety but the connective tissue that joins us to particular others, providing emotional safety to evolve. Having this secure base helps contain the longing we all have to belong, to be a part of something, to feel safe physically and emotionally, building the foundation for the affiliative and caregiving systems of being cared about, heard, understood, reassured, and validated. Without this, it's hard to ground in the body or open the heart.

What happens, though, when we aren't the lucky recipients of the relational lottery? The best news is that it does not mean we're stuck!

Research consistently reinforces that we can "earn" this inner secure base. Even if we didn't have the basics in place, we are designed as human beings to grow, develop, and become more. That drive is something we see in every age. On the playground a child might stay close to a caregiver while they assess what's out there, what the others are doing. At some point that wish to be part of—to play—takes over.

The researcher Trevarthen noticed that a child takes two to three forays away from the caregiver before they actually launch out into a new part of their world. Something will come up that makes the child want to return to safety. We see that any time we step outside our comfort zone. Outside our comfort zone we are less in control; we're less comfortable with the unknown. Inevitably some anxiety, worry, or fear will arise.

Until we know how to traverse that turbulence, we turn back toward safety, moving away from the anxiety and back into the proximity of safety. If we're received with care, attention, understanding . . . ahhhh . . . our system relaxes, eases. We replenish ourselves until we're ready to step back out outside our comfort zone again.

This cycle is how we begin to stretch our comfort zone, opening it, furthering the areas of life that we feel comfortable in. This native desire to explore leads us to the edges of our comfort zone. We balance our curiosity with fear that "It's not safe!" "Watch out!" "Bad things will happen!" With appropriate encouragement and support, we learn how to navigate this in-between phase of staying with the known while venturing into the unknown. What helps is knowing there are others who are there if something goes wrong. That knowing brings relief, allowing us to consolidate our learning, giving us a platform to continue risking stepping into the unknown, developing the confidence that we'll find our way through the unknown, knowing how to reach for support and learn from the experience.

That theoretical framework made sense when I saw what happened with children, most obviously, and less visibly with all adults. When a child is crying, raising her arms—she wants something. Most basically, she wants to be picked up, to be close, to be reassured, comforted.

So normal, right? Sitting with that in my own body, I realized that process isn't just physical. Or maybe a better way to say it is that accompanying the physical gesture is usually some of kind "attachment cry," an unspoken need. The physical movements were an indication of something else—some need the child has, needs we all have. This need to be comforted and reassured is absolutely normal to every one of us. Everyone has them! We can't escape them even though some of us may try to deny it.

This is our common humanity. We all share these primary basic needs of a secure attachment. Now let's tie in how these fundamental needs fit into attachment theory—specifically John Bowlby's internal working model which describes the perceptual lens out of which we relate to the world.

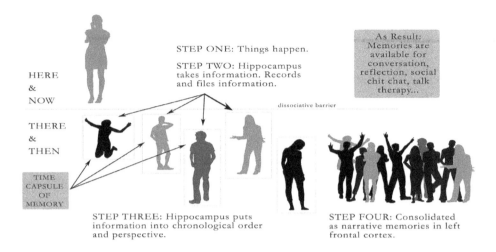

STEP ONE: Things happen.

STEP TWO: Hippocampus takes information. Records and files information.

HERE & NOW

As Result: Memories are available for conversation, reflection, social chit chat, talk therapy...

THERE & THEN

dissociative barrier

TIME CAPSULE OF MEMORY

STEP THREE: Hippocampus puts information into chronological order and perspective.

STEP FOUR: Consolidated as narrative memories in left frontal cortex.

How do you see the positive when something difficult happens? It's hard, right? Most of us fall into the automatic negative loops that we've gotten really good at. Self-compassion becomes difficult when we're suffering. Yet, rapidly expanding research demonstrates self-compassion is a means for easing body/mind/heart and building a foundation for wisdom, strength, and courage by "antidoting" pain. It forms a bridge between attachment theory and traditional meditation, allowing us to be with the pain of life without separation.

The brain is designed to do specific tasks. The most evolutionarily necessary one is to detect threat and take rapid action. Whole series of brain systems are dedicated to processing threat. If we're not careful, the automatic nature of the threat system will insidiously take over. Think of your day. Let's say you interacted with ten people, but there was one that was snide, or dismissive, or rejecting, and you got triggered. At the end of the day, as Paul Gilbert would ask, which of those people will you be ruminating about? Invariably, the one negative event.

Rick Hanson describes this as our being Velcro for the good and Teflon for the bad. Self-compassion provides the antidote. Self-compassion, as defined by Kristin Neff, researcher at the University of Texas, Austin, is designed to counteract the self-criticism we have, instead cultivating warmth and understanding toward ourselves when we make mistakes, fail at something, or feel inadequate.

So many people haven't had the good fortune to be surrounded by others who see the best in them, validate, reassure, comfort, guide, and protect them. As a consequence, when our protest hasn't been attended to by ourselves or others, we cascade into painful states.

When we take the time to be with ourselves in self-compassionate ways, the research shows we have more motivation, lower levels of anxiety and depression, and reduced self-criticism and self-judgment.

Christopher Germer, in his book *The Mindful Path to Self-Compassion*, identifies five ways we can increase self-compassion: spiritually, physically, mentally, emotionally, and relationally. If we weave that into the attachment orientation, we can think of it as an antidote to protest. When you're upset about something, ask yourself, "What do I need?" What does your body or your heart need?

Do you need to feel safe—internally and/or externally?

Might you want some attunement to what's going on inside? If there's no one available who can do that, how might you build an internal bridge of attunement? Listening inside, sensing what you need?

Perhaps you're needing reassurance, some kind of soothing to bring forth calm? You might have made a mistake that ricocheted and feel bad about it? What would help shift that?

Maybe you're feeling unseen? Or burdened by a lack of self-worth?

It might be you're needing someone to help you make sense of everything?

During times when we're caught in relational upheavals, we need support in dealing with the conflict, finding a way to repair the rupture.

How can I offer myself a tiny, thimbleful of the warmth I'm looking for? Or the attunement I need? So often, it's a need for reassurance, calming, and soothing.

EXERCISE: SELF-COMPASSION BREAK

Kristin Neff designed the Self-Compassion Break as a simple, yet powerful, practice to shift the stress caused by difficulty.

1. Becoming mindful. Acknowledge the suffering. Instead of plowing past what hurts, pause. Slow down. It can be as simple as saying to yourself, "This hurts." Or, "This is one of the ways I suffer." Acknowledging and validating what happened brings mindfulness right into the moment.

2. Common humanity. Like others, suffering is a part of life. I wish it were avoidable—for me, for you—but it isn't. This second step is a way to break the cultural miasma that we should always be happy, positive, or that something is wrong with us when something goes wrong. Instead, this second step acknowledges our common humanity. None of us get through unscathed. We all suffer.

3. Self-kindness. What do I need right now to express kindness to myself? Just like with *metta* practice, you're looking for the right phrase or gesture that gives you a sense of warmth or softens the intensity.

Shame as an Attachment Wound

Mary Ainsworth, Bowlby's colleague, described the fundamental developmental task in infancy as the establishment of a secure attachment. Later researchers elaborated that it includes a basic feeling of confidence in regard to the world, offering emotional regulation and impulse control, helping us grow into a person who can roll with life, without taking life personally, who can live within their emotional and physiological window of tolerance.

The basic function of welcoming our basic attachment needs is to help us build a solid, steady, secure inner core. As I talked about earlier, any time we step outside of our comfort zone to explore the world, some kind of anxiety is going to come up—some fear is going to come up. When the fear or anxiety comes up, what do we do? The normal, natural response is to reach for reassurance and comfort.

What happens if we don't get it?

What if instead of being reassured, we're shamed, humiliated, made fun of, ridiculed, or maybe even worse—ignored or shunned?

When our natural native need for comfort and reassurance is not met, our system inside is shocked. We're shocked. We don't know what to do.

Somewhere in our system we know it should be different, we "should" be getting a different response than we are. We can't make sense of it. It's disorganizing and disruptive; we become ashamed of the natural, normal hardwired needs that are part of the human condition.

From this perspective, we can see that shame is an attachment wound. A need arose—a normal, natural, primal need comes up inside. The normal cycle is that a need arises in order to be met; it's met, the cycle completes. When that cycle is interrupted or incomplete—when we didn't get what we needed—we feel like there's something wrong with us, since the need isn't met.

The more this happens, the more our native needs are not met, the greater the amount of shame we fall into. What's tragic about this is it happens on an almost biological level outside of reasoning. Our bodies convulse in shame, believing that there is something wrong with us—something critical that we didn't even know about.

Theoretical understandings and definitions may nicely summarize our cognitive understanding of shame . . . but nothing adequately describes the felt experience that comes instantaneously: It can feel like the whole body submerging into molten lava, burning every living cell inside. We may want to do anything to get away from the inner plunge into psychological chaos and horror. The body knows the experience first. Within nanoseconds, defensive responses come roaring online with the demand to hide, disappear, shut down. In the tightly packaged aftermath, the frontal lobe shuts down, information processing gets cut off. People often describe themselves at this point as blank, numb, or confused.

The tsunami of shame sets off every alarm bell in the body, igniting an intense cauldron of seething self-criticism, self-hatred, and every other painful self-attack. In the midst of reducing the self to smoldering shards, it's easy to miss the immense protest the heart is expressing: "It shouldn't be like this! This shouldn't be happening! NOOOO!"

Self-Compassion as an Antidote to Shame

When we're caught in the shame spiral, it's hard to step in and affect any cognitive intervention. Our bodies are caught in the emotional and physiological distress. However, the bridge between shame and repair is self-compassion. Caught in the shame spiral, physiologically overwhelmed by toxicity, naming and noticing begins to put a wedge into the spiral. "This is hard!" "This sucks." "This hurts." Instead of sliding further into pain, naming and noticing initiates the frontal lobe coming online again.

In my work with Frank Corrigan's Deep Brain Reorienting model, I've found it helpful to have people put a hand on the back of their head, making contact and connection above or near where the brainstem is located. This can help calm the highly active feeling states, providing a pause in activation. What a person needs in those moments is an environment of compassionate understanding, soothing, and reassuring. As we get into Parallel Lives in Skill 5, we'll look at how these imprinted painful past experiences rear their heads during shame spirals.

Once there's a little breathing room, the aftermath of shame needs to be connected in kindness—to know that we belong, that we're "a part of". We can do that with ourselves, reminding ourselves as Kristin Neff powerfully points out, we might not like what's happening, but we are suffering, just as so many suffer. It's through awareness of our common humanity that we shift the shame dynamic of being isolated, lonely, and cut off; instead we can find ourselves with like-hearted people who, like you, want to heal this pain and live a more satisfying life.

I've come to realize that healing these painful states is a modern-day bodhisattva training. A bodhisattva is someone who practices transforming suffering into

51

compassion. Doing the healing work you are doing is taking your painful life circumstances and deliberately learning how to do it differently, in a way that is more life-sustaining. Taking these steps increases your capacity to grow in benevolence inside, softening, and gentling the distress so that it's "right-sized."

This comes when we realize we can be with what is. Instead of protesting constantly, fighting against it or trying to get it to be different, we take the time to pause. If the protest is pointing the way . . . what do I need? How can I give that to myself in small, manageable ways?

This isn't about being passive, it's about staying with ourselves when life is difficult, aware of what we're going through, accepting the whole range of experiences without making any of them wrong. It's also about being able to respond and connect to life, instead of reacting against it, overwhelmed with anger, fears, anxiety, hopelessness or bitterness.

Super Powers of Transforming Shame

Power of Regret
In Buddhist and Sufi wisdom traditions there is this notion of the "power of regret." Regret is an immensely powerful tool. It acknowledges that we're sorry "this" happened. Instead of cascading into more and more distress, continuing cycles of pain within ourselves and with others, we "take the blow" without crumbling . . . and regret that it happened. This really requires that we are strong enough inside to not fall apart. It's a position of full responsibility. We can do this with ourselves for our own pain. We can regret that we were hurt. We can be sorry that any event or situation happened to us. We can also apply the power of regret to situations with others. When I've felt the grief and pain I've given to another, I'm open to a fuller experience of being sorry.

In doing this practice we'll encounter our own defensiveness. Someone will tell us that we hurt them and we'll find ourselves coming up with excuses and contexts to describe why we did it. In one of my coaching groups, Jenny reflected on how this happens in real time. How often, if someone points something out to us, do we take it as a personal offense?

The practice is actually something different. It's to take the "blow" and purify it with regret. Often for me, that means I have to stop, maybe take a breath, and not respond immediately. It might mean I allow the other person's words or experience to land inside me—to feel in me the effect I had on them. It is usually then that I feel a piece of their pain. It can feel like receiving an energetic, psychic blow. The defensiveness can be an immediate reaction to get away from that blow, to prove that I'm really not so bad.

It's very humbling at that moment to look up and say, "I'm sorry." "I regret that I did this." This can be a powerful practice. It's one which has radically altered my relationship to life. This kind of reflection is not about making ourselves feel bad, or ladling suffering onto suffering. It's about opening our hearts. It's about the simple act of kindness: "I'm sorry. I regret this is happening."

As we drop the story, drop the context around it, we sit in the power of regret that this is happening. This component building block of compassion creates space inside, cutting away the critical, judging mind, and allowing us to hold ourselves in our heart: I am sorry you are suffering. I'm sorry that I am suffering.

If someone is accusing us of being mean or neglectful, can we take the blow openly, pause, and explore whether there is a kernel of truth to it. This can be an uncomfortable and unwelcome practice, but it's the path of becoming non-defensive and compassionate.

REGRET REFLECTION

Where in your body do you sense regret? Is it in your body? Around your body?

_____

_____

_____

_____

_____

_____

What happens as you take on a stance of humility and openness? Perhaps slightly bowing, or dropping down and "taking a knee" physically or figuratively?

_____

_____

_____

_____

_____

_____

How does your body "take the blow?" What happens when you let your body feel the impact, the repercussions of the experience if only a small amount?

_____

_____

_____

_____

_____

_____

Does this cultivate self-compassion?

_____

_____

_____

_____

_____

The Power of Welcoming Neediness

We could say there is a really, really bad "four-letter word" that causes most people to cringe: need. Actually, more specifically, what makes us really cringe is the adjective "needy." Have you ever had a positive moment when someone called you "needy?" When you look at others and find someone who is needy, how do you respond?

Our self-sufficient world rejects neediness. We've learned to shut down our needs. It's why I'm so passionate about creating a positive context for our needs. If we don't get those fundamental attachment needs met the end result is shame—that there's something wrong with me because I didn't get my needs met.

We protest against being vulnerable, terrified if someone knows how much we need them we'll be rejected again. There might be a fear of being humiliated for needing someone or something. When our attachment needs were not (are not) met, we're left with a hole in which shame burrows. To counter our vulnerability, we have all kinds of defenses and protections. We worry about others who show what we disdainfully say is their "neediness."

Yet their neediness—our neediness—is a function of the most normal things in the world. We should have had those needs met. We didn't. But we can now. It's about pivoting away from how dreadful it is to be needy—to have needs—and orienting and awakening our compassionate heart that recognizes we all need. And that need, if channeled, can actually be the rocket fuel that takes us where we want to go.

To be able to tolerate the pain we are in for being needy, and to be with open hearts when we feel regret, we can practice the power of reliance. It's helpful to have examples of people who have transformed their pain into compassion.

Buddhism relies on the power of what's called the "Three Jewels:" Buddha (the example of what's possible), Dharma (the teachings), and the Sangha (community). The Buddha is an example of what's possible. Like other iconic figures, they give us an example of what is possible. They point the way. Christianity points to the example of Jesus. Muslims turn to Muhammad. Each religion and spiritual tradition has its own profound exemplar. However, this isn't just a religious or spiritual phenomenon at all. It's about recognizing what you value, what's important to you, and relying on those qualities. It could be a family member, friend, or member of your community. It could be one of millions of people who have left an indelible and positive legacy.

I'm a strong believer that each of us have to reconnect with our soul—our true nature. We need to be fed by the streams of reconnection to what is meaningful to us. Perhaps you connect with the Buddha as a source of meaning, or perhaps you have other sources that nourish your heart and soul. It might be nature, a pet, a volunteer community, or a social justice group.

Shame in its intensity is an expression of protest. We're protesting being disconnected from the fundamental needs we know we should have fulfilled. Our body—our hearts—are saying this is wrong! This shouldn't be. Inherent in it is a need. The pain, the shame of whatever we're suffering with, orients us to where we want to go.

What do you need? How can you turn toward something more nourishing than the shame, the suffering you are in? What can you rely on?

Neediness Reflection

What values do you hold dear?

_____

_____

_____

_____

_____

How can you hold onto those values despite what happened?

_____
_____
_____
_____
_____

Is it possible to share with someone that feels safe as much or as little as is comfortable about welcoming neediness?

_____
_____
_____
_____
_____

What is the need you have right now? What symbolizes that as an example or in image or words? What happens as you turn toward that nourishing opposite?

_____
_____
_____
_____
_____

Power of the Nourishing Opposite

One of my greatest teachers—one that I rely on—is the geranium in my office. Every day I go into my office, I water it, and turn it so these beautiful leaves and flowers will be looking in my direction. The funny thing is: This geranium has a mind of its own. It knows what it needs and by the end of the day it's turned and looking out the window, reaching for the light, the warmth, receiving the life force that keeps it alive!

As I was sitting with someone, listening and holding the pain this person was expressing, I realized we all need what the geranium has. We need to be where we are, with what life brings, but also turn toward what nourishes us.

This learning is part of the vast yogic teachings. If you do a yoga posture turning one way your body will automatically want to turn in the opposite direction to balance you out. If we think about protesting, we're fighting against something. What is the opposite? And can it be more nourishing?

Cassidy, who was one of my coaching clients, found this uncomfortably difficult, but tried it on. She had been "accused" by some of her friends as being self-centered. She hated that "blow" to her self-image. As she sat with it, trying to listen as non-defensively as she could, she recognized how she did bring every conversation back to herself. Her friends felt there wasn't any room for them in the conversations.

When I asked her the simple question, "What are you needing?" her body started to shake with memories of being shamed for needing to be special. We took the time to work through the shame. I kept reminding Cassidy how normal it is to want to be special, to be seen, to have value. That helped her body and heart ease. What then, I asked her, would be a more nourishing opposite of "taking up all the space?" That question opened something new for her, about sharing space and being included, instead of being pushed away. She realized she was "pushing others" away in her need to be seen, but that actually meant no one was being seen—there wasn't room for everyone.

NOURISHING OPPOSITE REFLECTION

What are you protesting?

_____
_____
_____
_____
_____

What then would be the nourishing opposite of the protest? Might you have a sense of what the need is?

_____
_____
_____
_____
_____

Power of Imprinting the Promise

When we're in the thick of things, we need to deal with the suffering we're in. Many of us, though, once we're out of the mess of it, let the practice drift away. We need to imprint in ourselves the promise to not repeat in the future the behaviors that have caused us pain. This promise can be for the next hour or the next day. Sometimes we can promise not to repeat at all, ever, for the rest of our lives.

For the most part though, this is a practice we take on every day. It's a gentle, constant practice of remembering to regret, to rely, to practice the nourishing opposite, and to promise to be in deep relationship with these practices. We need this promise to complete all the others.

With this kind of aware foundation, our capacity for compassion becomes easier. These building blocks make it easier to peel open the layers of obstacles so that our true heart—our true being—can shine out from our nature.

Underneath the crustiness of our protections is the beauty that has never been blemished. This part of you radiates and glows with your true source energy. For many, when we're in the middle of our healing, we shy away from knowing this beauty. We can't believe it's real. We feel lost in all the things that are wrong with us and haven't worked out. Yet, underneath that, is our own unblemished nature.

As one of my meditation teachers, Gehlek Rimpoche, says, "You have to know that you are good. You have to recognize that you have a beautiful human nature within you. In order to be able to love yourself you have to care for yourself."

IMPRINTING THE PROMISE REFLECTION

What can you promise to hold onto today?

_____

_____

_____

_____

_____

What possibility is offered in the Nourishing Opposite? How might you be different if you consistently oriented toward this?

_____

_____

_____

_____

_____

Self-Compassion in Everyday Life

Safety and Safeness

The invitation here is to use self-compassion as a place to slow down, pause, and integrate. We need to acknowledge our natural need to be safe. This is something we share with all mammals—the need to physically move toward safety. When any mammal (us included) senses danger, there is an instinctual movement toward a warm protective being. It's our native orientation to find protection against danger. If we don't have external safety, we draw ourselves deep into our bones—we move away from our extremities, getting as far away from the perimeter as we can.

Practicing self-compassion can come up against some internal roadblocks. Some, in fact, don't like the idea of self-compassion, because they use self-criticism as a way to motivate themselves. Self-compassion can feel too soft or seem like a practice that will keep them stuck.

Paula, who was a staff member at an organization working on issues of racial justice, strongly objected to joining a Mindful Self-Compassion group I was teaching. She tried to be nice about rejecting the suggestion, speaking out forcefully that if she practiced self-compassion the world wouldn't get better, causing her to be stuck in pain.

We talked about how important the issues she was working with were. I also mentioned we needed a whole spectrum of skills to work with any issue. If we're working with political, cultural, and social issues like systemic racism, it helps to not just push against what's there, but to know where we're moving and what we're moving toward.

What Paula is grappling with is the importance of safety—knowing we're physically safe and that we can help others be safe. It has to do with knowing that we're safe, physically safe in this moment. Built into that idea is an additional component—safeness, or the ability to feel emotionally and psychologically safe. This is a complicated arena for many in our society whose internal and external worlds are battling with power dynamics, like people of color, the LGBTQ community, or those in relationships marred by domestic violence.

We need to push against what needs to be changed AND we need to clear our internal space, so we feel safe inside our own being. Sayla used self-compassion while she was in a violent domestic relationship as a way to step out of it. "I practiced self-compassion maybe thousands of times a day. Over and over I kept realizing how much pain I was in; how much I was suffering. At first, I was mad at myself for being a victim, being stupid. I was world-class at beating myself up.

When Deirdre first suggested trying self-compassion, I rejected it. What helped me try it was recognizing how much I needed help. Rather than beating myself up for that, I began to recognize how much I wanted to be safe, inside and out. I wanted comfort, kindness, and caring connections. That helped me take the steps I needed to get out of the destructive relationship I was in. It took a long time, but I'm grateful I did it."

Open and Close

Another important element is knowing that there is a natural rhythm in life—we open and we close. Everything in life rises, crests, and falls. That rhythm flows everywhere, including our inner world. We come into the world as infants, grow into teenagers, adults, and then eventually die. On a smaller scale, a song starts, develops, and ends. When we orient to this natural rhythm, we recognize the many times we open and how we shift into closing.

We see this with infants in the research of Ed Tronick. There's the intensity of the infant gaze that is entrancing. Yet, as with all contact, there are moments when the infant looks away as a way to modulate the experience. Caregivers do this as well. This movement toward and away is something Beatrice Beebe notes in exquisite detail as the rhythms of connection between infants and caregivers.

Our heart opens. Then there's a time to pause, integrate, and step back perhaps. Within ourselves and with others we can pay attention to the natural rhythm: We connect and then take a moment away, come back, flowing back and forth between opening and closing.

We don't always have to be open. In fact, sometimes life is too much and we need to be able to close and integrate. We can have so much intensity or information that our systems become over-stimulated. To balance that, we might need to pause and find a balance. We need a way to rest—to turn away from the stimulation. There are definitely times we might need to shut it all down, but wouldn't it be nice if we could find easier ways, or more gentle ways to close down?

Recognize

Life happens on multiple dimensions. Sometimes we're fully present to the moment, or fully involved in a book or movie, forgetting our everyday life. Then there are the times when the past comes in and takes over. Those moments when the past takes over are not usually happy times; they're when we get caught up in the distress that consistently seems to engulf us, or we're caught in a fight that seems to always happen and never gets better. These moments when the past comes up and takes over are perfect times to practice self-compassion. It might be as simple as putting a hand on our heart murmuring to ourselves, "This is so hard, this is so hard." In those moments can you slow down a bit and notice your hand on your heart, feeling the warmth that's there? Pausing the rest of life while you tend to yourself in this moment? Yes, this is hard. And you're right there with yourself. We'll go more into this in the section on Parallel Lives and Resolving Triggers.

Often, we're in the here and now, but the past seeps into the present moment. It's confusing—we're triggered—our inner experience shape shifts. Perhaps it goes from being positive or uplifted to scary or sad—suddenly, we're certain something bad will happen, we'll be disappointed . . .

This isn't necessarily an inappropriate reaction. There are helpful imprints from the past we experience in the present, but some recurring patterns are less useful. If we learn how to interact in a certain way, it's hard to shift that. We find ourselves doing that over and over again many years later. I'm thinking of a client of mine who grew up in a military family, loving, but strict. He was taught to say, "Yes, ma'am." It became so ingrained in him that he still says it to this day. Helpful or unhelpful pattern? That's up to the individual to flesh out.

Many of the deepest imprints are embedded in us in the early months of life, before narrative memory is developed at two-three years of age. Or we are imprint-ed when we are experiencing a lot of emotions without time, space, or internal structure to make sense of all the feelings. Or we are imprinted with frequent repetition, like my client saying, "Yes, ma'am." Or any one of us that tells ourselves repeatedly, "You're not worth it," "Nothing good will come of this," or "You're a phony." Any of those one-sided put-downs.

Nevertheless, these powerful experiences are imprinted on and in us, becoming a felt template of how we experience, see, and hear the world. These impressions become a perceptual lens through which we experience the world. As with Bowlby's Internal Working Model mentioned earlier, we're imprinted by the relationships around us between birth and three years of age. These relationships unconsciously shape HOW we see and experience what happens to us and the world around us.

As we'll see in Skill 5: Addressing Parallel Lives, the past sneaks up and intrudes our current moment, creating a ruckus. This is where we can learn how to titrate life experience—this isn't something many of us were taught how to do growing up. But learning how to digest life and regulate our internal experience is something that can be learned. It's like eating a hot pepper that gives us a big POP of sensa-tion, and learning how to describe that POP, using words to shape the experience, either in a positive way or a not-so-positive way.

The words you say to yourself about an experience shape it—now and in the future. If we keep saying this or that is terrible, that gets further imprinted in us. When something comes up with a lot of feeling or experience, I often tell people to use a phrase like this: "Whew. This is hard—now. Boy, if it was this hard in the past, when I had less skills, less capacity to understand and be with this, no wonder it was so big."

In this way, we create an overarching understanding, linking the past to the present: This is what it was like back then. It's like we've opened up a time capsule of experience and our bodies and minds become suffused with the body memories—the felt experience of something from the past—even though we're still here in this moment.

Part of the goal of titrating is learning to dip in/dip out—not being overwhelmed by experience, but instead learning how to slow down experience, so we can take one thimbleful of it at a time. Integrate that. Dip in again, get a thimbleful of experience, dip out, and integrate it.

Self-compassion helps us shift the suffering we're in by recognizing there are things we want instead of being in pain. We develop the courage to open to what we need and want. Over time, we find ourselves becoming determined to live close to what's true to us, coming into harmony with our hearts.

EXERCISE: WELCOMING AND INCLUDING— SO HUM/HAMSA

Objective: When life feels too difficult to handle, this adaptation of the So Hum (I am) practice offers a way to embody what we have separated ourselves from.

Instructions: Externalize whatever part or experience is feeling complicated, either through your imagination or by writing or drawing it on paper. Imaginatively or concretely place what you are externalizing wherever it feels safe—in the room or outside the room.

Using the mantra So Hum (I am), quietly sense into your spine, landing in your body, grounding in your feet, centering yourself. I am. So hum. Right now, you are here. Right here.

As you feel yourself in your body, open your attention to this externalized part or experience you have been exploring. Open your arms in a gesture of welcoming, yet only include as much experience as you're comfortable with. So Hum. I am this too.

Taking all the time you need, make contact with this externalized experience; hold a posture of welcoming whatever is there. So Hum. I am this too. Being true to your own timing, staying in contact inside your body, as well as keeping in contact with this other, slowly draw the energy toward you. So Hum.

This too is me. Continue to draw the energy to you as long as it feels comfortable. No need to push or force it to happen, keeping with an attitude of exploration and welcoming.

SKILL 3: INTERNAL INFORMATION FLOW: THOUGHTS/FEELINGS/ SENSATIONS

Objectives:
- Learn ways to safely make contact with the array of thoughts, feeling and sensations involved in most experiences
- Start building distinctions—to know a thought as a thought, a feeling as a feeling, a sensation as a sensation
- Discover the Bridge of Attunement
- Detect previously unnoticed, but habitual associations
- Increase the capacity to sustain awareness
- Create a platform for intervening in experience and deconstructing/disarming triggers

Learning to slow down opens a doorway to greater ease and comfort for living inside our own skin. It might be hard to imagine when we're so used to living as if the body and mind are separate. Alice Graham, a psychotherapist in Belfast certified in the BSE skills, described how she's able to use this as a doorway to listen for triggers by becoming aware of and distinguishing between thoughts, feelings, and sensations. As she attunes to her clients, she often notices how they can get caught up in their story, losing track of what's happening inside. We can all do this work.

This is the work of becoming attuned to the language of the body. Alice spoke of what she does when she sees someone's activation, "I simply draw attention to that, for example, your teeth clench as you mention your mother, or you close your eyes tight and turn away."

It's always wonderful to have a skilled therapist listening to us, helping us attune to ourselves. But even when we don't have that external attunement, our adult developmental task is to attune to ourselves. That's where slowing down is so essential, giving us the chance to make contact with ourselves, instead of getting caught in the story line—usually one we've said to ourselves (and others) many times before. Unlocking this pattern of interacting with our internal world orients us to a great deal more spaciousness and choice.

Most of us come to our healing work having been in a lot of pain or distress. Otherwise, we may not have the impetus to face this stuff! I get it. We all do. As I shared earlier, healing is an Olympian task—deserving of its own medals. It takes dedication, commitment, and courage. And, unlike the glory of the Olympics, for most people this compassionate work is done in the quiet, humble background, without notice and with precious little signposts that we're changing.

When we can intervene in the pain and shift the suffering, we can feel a huge sigh of relief. When we recognize that we're triggered and realize we can do something to stop the spiral into horror, then we feel the sense of agency, that we're not subject to the constant barrage of suffering. Shifting this reactive pattern is the beginning of building a solid, secure, steady self.

Which is why we start with these basic practices as the crux of the healing work we must do: acquainting ourselves with the small building blocks of experience, the thoughts, feelings, and sensations that move rapidly within us. This gives us a greater awareness of what's happening inside the body at any given moment, which is necessary in the healing process. It provides an opportunity to intervene in the traumatic reaction and increases the possibility that we can shift what goes on inside in a more helpful direction.

"There is so much percolating under the surface," notices Kimberley Hopwood, a therapist in Victoria, BC, who trains therapists in a neurobiological approach to using the BSE skills with couples. "What's amazing is when we get into "body time," what the body wants us to work on is often different (but related) to what the person comes in the door having on their mind, or what they thought they'd want to talk about in their session."

Long-accepted habits of mind and emotion, as well as old holding patterns in the body, can easily hijack attention and pull you into past interpretations and associations, without your even being aware of it. We're so used to life being a certain way that we don't question it.

Bridge of Attunement

When we're in the old familiar way of being, these old associations are not easily distinguishable from the truth of the moment. We might not easily realize how much the pain we're in is linked to the painful stories we've been unconsciously repeating. Those patterns have come to represent our entire truth. When our frontal lobes are flooded with negative feelings or sensations, it is exceedingly difficult not to *be* the feeling.

Let's consider a toddler who is beginning to make sense of the world. This toddler looks around, interacting with people and objects, all of which stimulate what Daniel Stern, MD, called "vibrational affects." If we slow down the moment enough, we drop underneath the "stuff" of life to experience what's going on. Eugene Gendlin, the founder of Focusing, uses the word "felt experience" to access this state.

You know those times when you've seen dust moving slowly in the air? You can label it as "dust" (which would be naming and noticing), but what if you let go and let yourself experience a speck moving languidly? What happens in your body?

The experience comes first . . . and then we build a range of associations and interpretations around it. If I'm really curious and flowing in the felt experience I could reach for the speck and notice what happens as I do so—inside me and outside.

Most of us though, in our busy worlds, no longer see those little moments. They've become so familiar to us that we either overlook them or have shortcut language for them ("Oh, there's so much pollen in the air . . . ").

The toddler, however, lives in this felt experience, being with what happens as it happens. If there's someone there to help them make sense of their inner world, they can put pieces into place. We have the story of Helen Keller, who was deaf and blind from nineteen months old, who was caught in a world of inner chaos until her teacher Anne Sullivan helped her make sense of it. The first word Helen learned was w-a-t-e-r when Anne held Helen's hands under a pump's running water. Now water made sense. Water was this thing that flowed and was connected to quenching thirst, which the body naturally has.

If we didn't have someone help us make sense of our inner world, attuning to us, responding to us, interested in what happens inside, or even distinguishing between hunger and needing to have our diaper changed, we wouldn't know what to do with that mess of internal pulsing, vibrating, squiggling, shifting, or cramping.

As we grow up our brain develops; we learn to think, respond, and react, but for many of us, it's disconnected from our inner world. We build a self on top of that inner pulsatory world, using the words of Susan Aposhyan, the Boulder-based body psychotherapist.

Without that early attunement, our task is to build a "Bridge of Attunement": a self-connection, where we are in our own awareness while also attuning to these inner states as a means of making sense of what's going on inside. This ability is one of the fundamental adult developmental tasks we have to build, in order to have a solid sense of self inside.

As we've already explored, mindfulness, *metta,* and concentration practices are an important practice for dealing with upsetting mind-states. Just practicing these alone, however, are usually not enough. It's important to better understand and link together the sensations, the feelings generated, and the thoughts that roll rapidly through our heads.

To develop greater awareness and insight, we begin to recognize the thoughts, feelings, and sensations that form or provide context to our inner experiences. There's a hidden benefit, which comes when we explore the basic building blocks of experience: thoughts, feelings, and sensations. All of these can be studied, noticed, and explored. The more familiar and defined those internal distinctions are, the easier it will be to shift from old habits to new behaviors.

Maria cited two instances of how sitting with the discomfort produced by body sensations allowed her to shift her energy and awareness.

The first one happened while driving to meet a family member for a big holiday dinner; the muffler on Maria's car broke. Although she was scheduled to meet her siblings within the hour, she paused and let herself slow down, taking time to not just feel her anxiety and the worry that her family would be upset, but to recognize how her thoughts created fears, building anxious feelings, which usually trapped her in overwhelming sensations—all of which kept her from wanting to be in her body!

Using what she was learning in the BSE online course, she shifted. Instead of letting her worries run amok, this pause allowed Maria to slow her thoughts down so she could remain grounded in the moment and initiate positive self-talk. Her muffler was repaired quickly, and she was soon on her way. Maria later reflected on how proud she was of herself, and she remarked how the problem fortuitously occurred near a car repair shop. She was able to see the best in the situation.

Maria's other example occurred during a family visit that involved some "drama." She was able to sit through her discomfort and remain logical. Rather than call a friend to vent, she observed, "I could feel things swirling around inside of my core, activated because I had chosen a different behavior. Many parts of me weren't used to this approach! Instead of running away or shutting down, I took time to slow down and be with what was happening. I let it rise, crest, and fall. It eventually calmed down inside, just like you say, Deirdre, it moved through without me having to resort to all those old coping mechanisms I had."

Thoughts can be helpful or can make life more difficult. What we think directs our inner world, which is why Cognitive Behavioral Therapy (CBT) can be such a helpful tool to use. In using and developing our capacities to inquire what goes on inside, we can welcome and hold the emotional flooding and physiological sensations that otherwise might overwhelm our experiences.

In the brain, this happens in our cortex with our executive functioning, putting our chaotic inner world into order. Joseph LeDoux's work on fear helps us understand what happens when we get overwhelmed: Our thinking gets hijacked by having more neural connections from the amygdala firing alarm than there are connections from the cortex calming the amygdala. I'm sure you've had the experience of getting triggered and then finding it took a much longer time to calm.

At the same time, though, thinking can be helpful. We can use this ability to notice what's going on and name our reactions and responses to provide structure (which allows us to safely practice).

For example, I've had clients who become so distressed when their history erupts that they feel unable to go to work. I remember the day my client, Misha, came into the office, wanting to take disability from her job in finance. My heart broke for her—for the intensity and disruption of her experience. I also knew how much a helpful structure could help keep someone out of the constant rumination. I invited Misha to slow things down, literally using her work—her focus on numbers and balance sheets—to focus her mind and create an internal container for her body. It helped. She was grateful not to lose the income, but more than that, she grew in self-respect as she began to master her crazy inner world.

Using our cognitive capacity helps when we know we're going to go into a provocative situation. We can think ahead and strategize how we'll handle the situation. Or we can take previous experiences and deconstruct them, exploring new ways to handle them in the future. This can help us deal with the unexpected, instead of being swept under by them. Engaging in intentional and mindful anticipation is akin to developing a muscle that can help arrest our descent into habitual self-shaming behaviors.

Skillful thinking also helps to develop distinctions among shifting ego states. Usually when a person gets flooded and overwhelmed, we are no longer experiencing the facts of the moment; rather, the experience has become a tangle of sensations, feelings, and thoughts. Moreover, the present experience typically has merged into a previously undigested experience (see Skill 5: Addressing Parallel Lives for additional information).

Mastering this de-lumping-together of experiences creates a sense of clarity and control. The fundamental inquiry whenever one is faced with an overwhelming state is whether or not the experience feels out of proportion to what is happening.

Here's something to take note of: If it's too big for this moment (too charged), and we feel lost in it, then you can assume it's fueled by a painful past association.

In this way, thinking while using appropriate distinctions helps us to navigate difficult experiences and eventually allows us to move in a desired direction.

There are, however, times when we don't use thinking skillfully. We can get caught in common hurdles like:

- *Over-analyzing* which occurs when we use thoughts without regard to sensate or affective information provided by the body. The obsessive aspect prevents anything new from entering the loop of repetitive analysis, leading a person further from the reality of the moment.
- *Distancing* which prevents direct experience when we conceptualize what we think is going on, instead of having ourselves explore what is truly there.
- *Negative associations to, and negative predictions of* internal experiences are often involved.

In general, all cognitive distortions discussed in Cognitive Behavioral literature are examples of unskillful thinking.

Feelings is the general term I'm using for the emotional experiences we go through. Like thinking, our feelings must be balanced with other aspects of experience.

Talking about feelings with trauma survivors evokes mixed responses! Often feelings are experienced as overwhelming, unrelenting, painful episodes. They can completely take over the sense of self.

Feelings, particularly in the early and middle phases of healing, might be highly charged, difficult to be with, and many try to avoid them if at all possible. If we can analyze the myriad layers of experience contained in a word like "sadness," we can recognize the encoded associations and interpretations, instead of solely reacting to them. This help us feel less controlled by these feelings, giving us access to use them as valuable clues to explore and expand our sense of self.

Deepening understanding of our psychological selves provides access to use our feelings more skillfully. For instance, we might recognize feelings as messages from repressed parts of ourselves, informing us about something in the here and now, or revealing how the past is leaking or gushing into our present moment.

Being in touch with feelings is important and necessary. Feelings provide important signposts about our likes and dislikes, fears and hopes, and help us to identify our safety boundaries. Since being in a physically safe environment and having a safe internal experience is critical in healing trauma, people need to know the inner signals that indicate safety to them.

Feelings also provide contrast, helping us reject the current undesired state, and create momentum for finding a preferred alternative.

Avoiding feelings can interfere with becoming embodied. When our internal world feels treacherous, it's hard to explore our inner landscape. In failing to relate to our feelings, we can perpetuate a fractured relationship to the self that is defined by chaotic episodes induced by painful triggers. Avoiding this vicious cycle requires us to discover how to befriend ourselves and our feelings.

Feelings sometimes get in the way because they can be so mismatched to the reality of a situation that they lead to misguided actions, thoughts, or plans. In those times, the feelings are a signal that the past is intruding into the present moment, projecting onto our experience. When we learn to welcome feelings as a guide, linking our present with our past, we can use the information wisely.

When you are over-immersed in feelings, you might shut down from exploring possibilities. You might not be able to accept new ideas about where you want to go and who you want to become. Instead of being creative, you may remain paralyzed or avoidant, stuck in old ways of being. Perpetually overwhelming feelings dictate a protective, constricted, and numbed-out life. Such a state makes it seem impossible to live a happy and satisfying existence. Chaotic feelings can prevent the marshaling of resolve and the necessary focusing of energy to achieve a different, more positive outcome.

My coaching client Philippe ran into this conundrum. Like others, he had been told repeatedly that his feelings were invalid. Having been shut down by others for so long, he wanted to regularly explore his vulnerable, shaky feelings to access his "true self." Not having been attuned to, Philippe argued for his feelings. But wanting people to attune to the depths of every emotion was keeping Philippe from moving forward in his career. So, he learned to attune to himself, validate what he was feeling, and reassure himself, instead of demanding others do so. Not only did that make life easier for him, but his wife felt she wasn't always having to be so highly attuned to his emotional needs that she was burning out.

Body sensations can be particularly challenging for people who have experienced trauma, but they are a critical element of creating ease in the body. If we don't trust our bodies to be inviting places to visit, then we probably have had limited positive experiences with body sensations.

Sensations are the basic building blocks of embodied experience. When we experience physical sensations—such as tingling, tightening, loosening, vibration, warmth, cold, movement of some kind—we often have an unconscious and automatic response. As these sensations are often clustered, they can be interpreted many different ways, depending on the associations we've previously made to and with them.

As soon as we experience a sensation, we are almost immediately importing some association or story from the past, or a prediction about the future, that we superimpose onto the current moment. In this state, we rarely experience what is truly happening at that moment; rather, we revert to old interpretations, predictions, or stories of what we believe to be true. Although oversimplified, the associations and stories for trauma survivors can be extremely distressing.

Isolating body sensations offers tremendous benefits. Most sensations are not necessarily pleasant or unpleasant. A tingle is a tingle; muscle movement is just that; trembling is just trembling. That is, until we introduce a belief that associates those sensations with a problem. If sensations are interpreted through past trauma, typically innocuous sensations can become problematic. For example, we can associate trembling with crying, crying with fear, and fear with imminent danger. We create a nanosecond shorthand: A simple sensation is equated with danger, whether danger is present or not.

Isolating single sensations within a cluster reduces stress in the body since there's less information to process. People who suffer from panic attacks are often relieved when they focus on single sensations, such as the heart beating, instead of attending to how hard or fast it's beating. Notice just the beat . . . beat . . . beat. When we identify individual sensations, we limit the information we must process, which helps interrupt the feeling of being hijacked by all the attendant associations that usually accompany the panic attack.

When we remain present with pure sensation, we are focused in the moment and are open. The possibilities of interpreting the moment have been expanded, as the connections with painful stories and associations from the past have been loosened.

An unbalanced focus on sensations can present problems, particularly when sensations seem to appear out of the blue. Caught unaware and lacking the appropriate tools, we may feel out of control. In this case, sensations present themselves as an overwhelming, chaotic mass of stimulation. At those times, it can feel like slowing down sensations is impossible. They roll through so quickly we can't isolate them, let alone name them in a mindful way. At those times, we might find ourselves doing almost anything to shut off—numbing, blanking out, or acting out are common responses.

Usually when sensations are clustered together and contain unnoticed and unchecked associations to the past or future, they become overwhelming and unbearable.

Opening to pure sensation is an effective means to bring us into the present, but we have to be aware that we might, at times, also find the experience too expansive, too open, or too devoid of boundaries.

People unconsciously create a sensate shorthand as we age. Studying and exploring each sensation takes time and practice. When we take the time to become aware, we are more likely to skillfully intervene as stress levels increase.

After years of journaling without affecting any change, Roberta, while reading Becoming Safely Embodied, learned to identify her thoughts, feelings, and body sensations. She noticed that her stomach was the locus of all her emotions, feelings, and sensations, from which they cascaded to other parts of her body. Once she focused her attention on her stomach as the starting point, she realized that none of what she was feeling was threatening. Then she focused on her thoughts—first on one, and then as many as three at a time. By doing so, she found that she could think more clearly and no longer felt herself escalating into panic-mode.

EXERCISE: WHAT'S ANXIETY LIKE IN THE BODY?

To illustrate the preceding points, let's explore the sensation of anxiety, a common state for many. What sensations are present in your body when you're anxious?

To give you a bit of prompting, the list generally includes fast heartbeat, butterflies, muscle constriction, difficulty breathing, shallow breathing, muscle movements, and agitation.

Now compare those notions of anxiety to excitement. If I were to ask you, "What sensations do you experience when you are excited?" Generally, most people cite muscle impulses, butterflies, rapid heart rate, shallow breathing, and agitation.

So, I wonder with you, what's different?

The answer is: The context and association—the label placed on the cluster of sensations. Until we learn to distinguish individual sensations, feeling numb and having shallow breathing will be the stimulus to anxiety, inciting us to keep our distance from experience, rather than viewing it as an opportunity for deeper self-examination.

Jessica consistently had an experience of being shut down, saying, "I really struggle with identifying my feelings. When I slow down . . . I just notice that I feel numb. And I think maybe this is because I am being so overwhelmed, my body shuts down." Over time, with practice, she came to realize, "Dropping into my experience wasn't easy. I never knew what to expect. I didn't know what would be there, and often it felt like there was nothing. I would feel numb or shut down. Deirdre suggested I watch how I would subtly dismiss a thought, feeling, or sensation, or avoid it completely—not wanting to get any closer to it. I began to practice making room for everything, slowly and gently, welcoming whatever was there, and in this case, it was often numbness. I started acknowledging the state, the experience I was in: 'OK, I'm numb everywhere.' Deirdre would ask me to explore further, 'Is your earlobe numb? What do the hair follicles in your left eyebrow feel? What happens when you touch it? Does it feel like something's there? Can you feel yourself squeezing it?' I began to see that there were many places in my body that weren't numb. That gave me courage to explore a bit further, 'Is my jaw numb?' I would touch it. I would explore what it felt like from the outside, using my fingers, and notice what was happening inside when my fingers were touching it outside. I began to realize that not everything was numb. I could differentiate where I felt numb and opened to realizing there were parts of my body that felt alive, easy, relaxed—even at peace. Now I ask myself: 'What does numb feel like? What is the experience of being numb? When I'm numb, what are the thoughts I have? What are the feelings I'm having? What are the body sensations? How long does numbness last? Is the numbness everywhere? Where does it start and stop? Can you expand or shrink the numbness?' I've been grateful to get to know my body in this way, dropping the labels I have. It's through cultivating curiosity about what goes on inside that I can feel my entire life change."

Meditation and Complicated Experiences

For interested readers, I want to explore some of the Buddhist meditation, which undergirds the BSE concept. The Buddhist approach to working with difficult emotions has some interesting applications for working with entrenched emotional dysregulation.

The first application provides an antidote when a person is feeling caught in a negative emotion. If one is feeling anger or hatred, it may be impossible to feel love/kindness/softness. The remedy is to soften into the experience, or "lean into it," as Pema Chödrön says, to help open up the moment. Someone filled with jealousy might discover an antidote by intentionally appreciating something about that other person. If we're angry at another, it might help us relax inside if we acknowledge that "so and so often might be mean to others, but they treat their aging pet really well." It's a simple practice, yet requires tremendous intentional focusing.

For trauma survivors whose feelings might be fueled by compartmentalized and regressed parts, finding an antidote becomes much harder. If those feelings were traumatically encoded at age five, we begin to understand the complications: A young angry, hurt, or despairing child doesn't have the psychological capacity to shift gears and soothe herself.

For adults with a trauma background, cultivating the antidotes can be a powerful practice. It includes welcoming everything, making space for all feelings, thoughts, and sensations. In the Internal Family Systems model, we say all parts are welcome.

Over the years, I have met innumerable trauma survivors who have rich spiritual practices. Through diligence they have learned to cultivate states of mind that provide equanimity, sympathetic joy, loving kindness, and compassion (the heavenly abodes of the mind, or *brahma viharas)*.

Even with a developed spiritual practice, however, most trauma survivors eventually find they need to tend to the trauma held in psychological aspects of mind, which have been compartmentalized. Because mindful states feel better, many trauma survivors have been drawn to a spiritual path to avoid dealing with their still incomplete and often disruptive history. As beautiful as these cultivated states may be, by themselves they can become another way of compartmentalizing and keeping life at bay.

Instead, trauma survivors must learn to stabilize their mindfulness and compassionately enter these regressed states. This takes concentration—a willingness to keep focusing on where you want to go, even as that regressed part is howling and yelling at you, going blank, or pushing against you. This kind of concentration includes mindfulness, which creates an ability to penetrate these rising states of overwhelm and see these states for what they are.

The capacity to note and to witness here is critical. If we can see what's happening and slow down the overwhelm, we can carve out new internal territory. Applying this newfound gentleness and softness provides us with a type of psychological safety net. As dual capacity is cultivated (i.e., being able to be in this moment while simultaneously observing what's happening), people stay more anchored in the present moment. They develop the necessary self-structure to tolerate distress and can witness regressed material with equanimity and compassion. In fact, in many traditions, the word meditation means *familiarization.* Through the practice of meditation, clients familiarize themselves with these tortured states of mind, thereby releasing the pain long associated with those triggers.

By weaving the antidotes together and increasing familiarity with these challenging states of mind, individuals can shift their attention more skillfully. The more often they find their way to inner domains of peace and safety, the more trust and courage they engender within themselves, the more likely they will safely encounter these heavy emotional states. The more often they mindfully encounter this inner turbulence, the less likely they are to be surprised and derailed by those states. Clients can learn to alternate between a willingness to mindfully explore what's present (even when it's not pleasant), and a concentrated practice to focus the mind, body, and heart on what you want to attend to, thereby scaling back overwhelm and countering habitual negativity.

The next step is learning to find the appropriate antidote in meditation. With a meditation practice, one begins to see the inherent nature of upsetting states as less solid and less fear-inducing than previously thought. The more consistently we practice shifting our internal experience, the more natural it becomes to adopt that more constructive behavior, that new habit of sage intervention, when things are falling apart. A baby step toward developing that kind of mindfulness is to become aware of the T/F/S (thoughts/feelings/sensations) that intertwine and coalesce into upset. As we begin to name the T/F/S that constructs our realities, we begin to see/know how they are distorting our reality.

TWO EXERCISES TO DISCOVER INTERNAL INFORMATION FLOW

Exercise 1: Standing in the Mountain

While holding the "mountain" yoga posture for ten to fifteen minutes, or another more comfortable posture, report everything going on in your mind and body.

If you have a safe other, have them take notes of what you are saying and any nonverbal or physical responses (such as arms dropping, feet shifting, shaking or trembling, and so on). You can always ask your partner to trade with you, so they can take a turn afterwards!

Once you've milked the experience, take a deep breath and as you exhale, slowly lower your arms, taking time to notice and report what's happening as you return to the starting posture. Describe or journal the experience of relaxation. What words come to mind when you are in your body and can savor that relaxing experience? What thoughts, feelings, and sensations were you aware of, and if you did this with a partner, what did they notice? Were you able to notice how behaviors shifted with any changes in your internal dialogue?

_____

_____

_____

_____

_____

What did you learn? What was your takeaway from this experience?

_____

_____

_____

_____

_____

Directions for the Mountain Posture:

Come to a standing position with your feet hip-width apart. Take a moment and notice what the ground feels like. You may want to shift your weight as you stand, noticing what position feels most grounded to you. Roll onto your toes and back onto your heels, or sway side to side. Come to a sturdy and balanced position. Bring your attention to your whole body; inhale and press up into the crown of your head. You might feel your head lift and your spine elongate. Simultaneously, press gently up into your crown and down into your feet. Notice the lengthening sensation.

Then begin to gently press down into your fingertips. You'll notice as you do that, there's a pull along your shoulders. If possible, also press up into your crown. Take a deep breath, and press down into your fingertips; slowly raise your hands up along your side. As your hands reach shoulder-height, rotate your palms upward.

Press your shoulders down and raise your arms straight up overhead. Pause when your palms face each other directly above your shoulders. Take a long, deep breath. Relax your shoulders; press down into your feet and up through your crown. Let your bones—your structure—hold you in position, keeping your muscles relaxed and your breathing easy.

Exercise 2: Walking Toward

This is a version of a walking meditation. Choose an object that you can place in front of you. It might be a pillow; it might be a chair. It could be the book or tablet you're reading.

Find an object around you that you can use to focus on. I want you to use an object that is not something unpleasant, but something that has more of a positive feeling or a neutral feeling. We're literally going to take baby steps, one step at a time. If you can't stand and walk, then just do this from a seated position and just see the object nearby.

As you stand or sit there with this object nearby, just see what happens in your body. Notice what is there. If you're like most of us, in any single moment there are multiple thoughts and feelings and body sensations going on. Some of you might say, "Well, I feel numb. There's nothing there." Then I want you to just notice what that numbness is and stay with that or stay with the other feelings that are there.

Take one tiny step forward toward your object, whatever it is. Then stop. Just that one step. Notice what happens in your body. Notice the thoughts that are there, the feelings. And the feelings are going to be different from thoughts. And the body sensations. Body sensations are going to be things like tingling, warmth, shakiness, or fluttering. Those are the basic building blocks of a sensation.

Then, notice if there are any feelings that go with any of those sensations. Or see if you can stay with the bare sensation. You might have a lot of thoughts that happen, as well.

Then, take another small step forward toward your object. Again noticing; not making anything right, anything wrong. Just noticing your experience.

If you have a lot of feeling or a lot of sensation going on, see if you can narrow the focus into one particular sensation. Bring your attention right to whatever is calling it, letting any thoughts and feelings go, just staying with that one sensation.

And if you have a lot of thoughts like, "This is really stupid. This isn't working. Why am I doing this? These things never work for me . . . " **welcome them**

all. Don't try to make the thoughts right or wrong. Notice them. Let them exist by themselves and see if you can notice how many thoughts you have in one tiny second.

Then, take another step—a small step. See if there are any feelings that are there. Breathe into whatever is there, noticing what is showing up in this walking meditation.

You may notice that the more you slow down the moment and take one little step at a time, the more you're going to be aware of your different experiences.

Stay with your body and notice what thoughts are there, what feelings are there, and what body sensations are there.

Checking the Results of the Exercise

What did you notice? If you felt there was nothing there, what is the experience that goes with nothing being there? Even numbness can be decoded and understood. Often when we say, "Well, I didn't feel anything," Is that a thought? Are there any feelings going with that thought? What happens in your body when you say, "I don't feel anything?"

- Is it across the board?
- Is there no place in your body that you feel anything?
- Can you feel something in your baby toe? Or if you touch your finger to another finger, what do you feel there?
- What's a body sensation that goes with that numbness? We can start inquiring deeper and deeper into what's going on.

The object we choose is actually meaningless. We're using the object to awaken our inner experience. We're looking to see what thoughts we are having about that object. To focus on what T/F/S we're experiencing in the moment . . . and then to slow it down even further, to see what just the sensations in your body are.

Example One:

Marian: It's a silly eyeglass holder.
Deirdre: Is there a thought that goes with that?
Marian: Yes, this is stupid.
Deirdre: Are there any feelings there as well?
Marian: Well, there was that thought. And it's a judgmental thought. Which I'm good at (laughs). And then when I really started to explore what was going on inside . . . I guess there's anxiety . . . Here I am, looking at this object that I like and I have positive

associations to, but what was really going on inside was that I didn't feel anything, but then noticed I was full of total anxiety and my heart was beating fast, like in my throat, fluttering in my chest, and something sort of—it crossed my mind quickly which was "Here all alone." So, I was looking at this thing but I think I noticed—anyway, it was just total anxiety.

I asked her if she wanted to explore this a bit more, which Marian was open to.

Deirdre: What happens in you when you look at the object with bare attention? (The word "silly" was a big clue that there was a lot going on inside!) What do you see as you see it?

Marian: Colors.

Deirdre: Is there one color you are more drawn to?

Marian: Purple.

Deirdre: Attend to and focus on that purple color. What happens in your body?

Marian: I breathe a little more. A little more space. I'm aware of my breathing now. I can feel myself calming down.

Example Two:

Alex: At first, I didn't notice anything. I couldn't tell if there were any thoughts, feelings, or sensations. So, I took a step away from my table. As I moved away, I found myself feeling anxious and trying to stay with that feeling alone. It was kind of weird because all I was doing was moving further away from my seat. I realized I was worrying and then had the thought, "Oh, this is a game!" Then I flipped into excitement because I love games.

Deirdre: What's so interesting, Alex, is you had the thought, "Oh, this is a game," and then that brought up all these other associations of getting excited about a game . . .

Alex: It was a real flip into excitement, yeah.

Deirdre: That's a great example of how our thoughts, or how we frame life, can impact our experience. We load our life experiences with associations, good and bad. "Oh, it's a game": I can be excited. If I'm near my safe place, maybe it's because I wasn't thinking life is scary and I have to stay close to my safe place. All those kinds of associations get stuck in it, whereas if you can stay right with your table and feel, or let your body feel the table, then maybe what you feel is smooth wood, right?

Alex: Uh-huh (Yes).

Deirdre: If you touch your table, what do you notice?

Alex: It's solid. And very, very dear.

Deirdre: That's right. When you feel it's solid what happens in your body?

Alex: Very grounded, like roots of a tree.

Deirdre: How does your body experience solid inside?

Alex: Hmmmmmm. I don't really have words for it . . . Let's see. Like I have a core? I feel my spine connected to my legs . . . feels really good, like I won't fall down.

Example Three:

Ann: I was aware of a number of sensations in my body. I didn't get any emotion, though. What I did was I felt things in different places, so I decided to focus on one. Like my upper abdomen was feeling really tight, so I started putting my attention on that and I started getting kind of like a spasm there. Then I kind of got the message that it didn't want to open.

Deirdre: So, you were mostly staying on the sensation level and then you got a message. Sounds like there was a thought that something inside didn't want to open?

Ann: Yeah. Well, like that muscle that I was focusing on didn't want to open.

Deirdre: What happens if you listen and trust that message?

Ann: Feels right. Kind of like I'm aligned inside. Like I can trust myself.

Deirdre: Those are the kinds of messages that can help guide us or help us know to slow down. Even if we're walking toward something, as you stop maybe there was some guidance on a sensate level that was like, "No, I don't want to take another step." And by listening to that, or whatever that tightness is, you found your own pacing, which allows you to tune into your own guidance.

Example Four:

Claudia: Again, I'm going to be really honest. When I first looked at my object, the window curtain, I was thinking, "This is stupid. This isn't going to help me. This isn't going to do anything." [Laughs] I noticed that as I was standing there, before I took the first step, there was judgment all over the place. "This is going to be another thing that's not going to help me. I'm too far beyond help. There's no way that I can overcome all of this. I'm just too far beneath all this stuff." I was just going and going.

And I looked at it; there was this hesitation to walk toward it. I kind of stopped and went, "Well, what's that about?" And noticing that and noticing my body and whatever. And then thinking, "Gosh, I wish it was this easy to be with my fears." I wished it was this easy. It was interesting because I found the closer I got, the less I was able to look at it, which like totally threw me. [Laughs]

Deirdre: And then what happened in your body? Because you had those thoughts going on about how stupid it was, and then you were noticing what was going on outside of you, what was the effect it had on your body?

Claudia: *Well, I guess one of—how do I say this—not in a panic but more of just I wanted to like shut down. I just wanted to run. Kind of just shut down. But not in a fearful way, more like, "Oh, don't pay attention to the feelings anyway because this isn't going to work." I'm being really honest. [Laughs]*

Deirdre: *I love that. You know, what you're modeling for all of us, Claudia, is the more honest we are, and the more real we are about our own experience, the more we're going to learn.*

Claudia: *I just—yeah. I just wanted to shut down.*

Deirdre: *That's right. That's right. And that's what we do. We see the curtains and the curtains become the negative association and it has an effect of wanting to shut down our body. If you look at this curtain, what color is the curtain? What shape is the curtain? If you just see it for what it is, without all the loaded associations, then your body can relax a little bit, because it's just a color or shape.*

Claudia: *Can I ask just one quick question before we move forward?*

Deirdre: *Sure.*

Claudia: *How do you do that with something that feels too big for us? When the experience is "This is just way too big and I'm just simply going to die from the fright itself" kind of thing. So, what do you do when it's not something, a single object that you can focus on, but something that feels way too big for you? Does that make sense?*

Deirdre: *Well, what you do is you start with a small thing. You start with a curtain or you start with another neutral object and you start seeing it in those moments. The more you know it in those small moments, the more you're going to be able to practice when the bigger things happen.*

Claudia: *But do you begin to notice the thing that you're fearful of, or do you just notice the things that are around you . . . like a sense of mindfulness?*

Deirdre: *I'd start with a sense of mindfulness first. I mean, the things that we're fearful of are big. We can easily get caught up in a negative loop. It's hard to stay centered and grounded when we're afraid. We literally have known that the research on the brain shows that there are more neural networks going from our medulla to our brain, from our limbic brain to our frontal cortex, than there are from our frontal lobe back down to our bodies, our limbic system. So, when we get activated, we're having a rush of material flood our frontal lobe, making it harder to calm down. You know when you get overwhelmed it takes longer for your body to slow down. Well, that's because literally in our body we don't have as many networks going from our frontal lobe down into our body.*

Internal Information Flow Reflection

Take a moment to jot down a few thoughts in response to the following questions.

Feeling words are those we use to describe clusters of experience and they tend to illustrate states of being. Words like "joyful," "sad," "angry," "disconnected," "bored," "refreshed," "startled," and "afraid" can all be traced to actual sensations in the body. Without even noticing, we can leapfrog over most of the actual experience when we say we "feel" something. Rather than wondering or investigating how we know what we're feeling, we jump to conclusions. For example, when you describe yourself as feeling "shy," how do you know that? What in your body tells you that?

_____

_____

_____

_____

_____

Sensation words are those that describe the physical experiences that make up feelings. For example, if I am feeling irritated, I might experience my muscles tightening—perhaps in my belly, chest, or jaw. There might be other sensations too, such as warmth or cold. See how much of your sensory experience you can describe. Also look for new words to describe the different sensations.

_____

_____

_____

_____

_____

What are you feeling right now? *Joyful, confident, relieved, glad, happy, pleased, flat, disconnected, bored, resigned, apathetic, angry, bugged, annoyed, rattled, ruffled, giddy, afraid, shy, startled, uneasy, tense . . . or something else?*

_____

_____

_____

_____

_____

Ask yourself how your body/mind lets you know what you are experiencing? What sensory information compels you to say, "Oh, I'm feeling. . ."

_____

_____

_____

_____

_____

Where is each sensation located inside your body? Watch to see if you are explaining where it is. Try to be simple and concrete (e.g., "It's in my arm, belly, chest, or face.")

_____

_____

_____

_____

_____

Try to distinguish the sensations that you're feeling. What words would you choose to describe what's going on? Pick some words from the list below OR add your own words to the list: _tingly, hot, cold, warm, tight, dull, shaky, numb, trembling, shivery, thick, tense, damp, congested, vibrating, sharp_ . . .

_____

_____

_____

_____

_____

SKILL 4: SEPARATING FACTS FROM FEELINGS

Objectives:
- To separate the facts of a situation from your habitual interpretations about those facts
- To begin seeing and mapping the internal terrain, encountering the "realities" people are prone to live out and finding out if there is any real evidence to support those beliefs
- To notice that the habitual sense of self and the actual self/potential self may differ
- For hyper-aroused clients to become calmer, and for numb clients to experience more contained energy

When there's been trauma, people tend to vacillate in what we call the biphasic trauma response. Pat Ogden, who started the Sensorimotor Psychotherapy Institute to help therapists learn how to process traumatic activation through the body, has a beautiful way to visualize and describe the triggered response. Whenever we can "tolerate" our experience, we are in our "window of tolerance" (Siegel, 1999). When we are outside our capacity to tolerate the life experience, we are either hypo-aroused (numb, shut down, blank, foggy) or hyper-aroused (anxious, terrified, overwhelmed) (Ogden, 2006). Our task is to increase our capacity to be with what happens in life, widening our window of tolerance. When we're inside the window of tolerance, we're able to handle life.

Here's a technology metaphor to help make sense of this. When the Internet first became widely available in the 90s, I had to use a dial-up modem to access my Compuserve account. I would click on the "You've got mail" button, and wait. And wait. It felt like an eternity for the few emails to download. There often was time to go downstairs, make a cup of tea, and read the paper. I'd then go upstairs, and if I were lucky, I'd have an email or two to look at.

You think I'm exaggerating? Not by much! Today, with gigabit-download speeds, some people receive their email and stream web services almost instantaneously. That's essentially what we want to do—to increase the bandwidth of our internal worlds . . . to learn to broaden our capacity to integrate material, so our lives can be richer and more fulfilling.

We each have different capacities to tolerate cognitive, emotional, and sensory experience. The more we can, the bigger our window of tolerance. The less information we are comfortable letting in, the smaller our window of tolerance. Of course, when we have more stress in our lives, we'll have less resources or capacity.

The experience most trauma survivors have is that they're not living in that window of tolerance, which doesn't mean that they don't have a window of tolerance, it's just that the hyper-aroused and the hypo-aroused ends are so strong and affectively emotionallyladen that they take a lot of attention. When hyper-aroused, over-stimulated with anxiety or stress, we will at some point become exhausted. To deal with that, we might want to numb out or collapse. To deal with overstimulation, we disconnect. It's an adaptive way to manage, but in the long term it doesn't produce a satisfying life.

Each of us will have a different subjective window of tolerance. It's important to get a sense of your starting point, so you can track how your window begins to expand over time and practice.

You may find, like so many, that being in your window of tolerance might actually feel boring—like nothing's happening. Let's think about it for a moment. If our bodies are so used to being hyper-aroused, and then we plunge into shut down (hypo-arousal) to deal with it, our bodies are used to the highs and lows of life. It will feel different to get out of that cycle. "Boring is good!" I remind my clients. It's good for the body to recalibrate, relax, rest, and replenish.

Given how important it is to get to know your own inner responses, take a moment to pause and notice:

Are you hyper-aroused, feeling anxious? Or maybe over-stimulated?

Or maybe you tend to be more hypo-aroused? Perhaps feeling flat? Do you feel numb? Do you feel disconnected? Depressed?

To help you sort this out, let's generalize a bit. Many people, when they're hyper-aroused, tend to use substances or activities to manage the activation, perhaps by binging one way or another. They might over-exercise, over-eat, over-drink, or use prescription meds or other drugs. Sex or porn can be outlets for people as they try to direct their energy.

What can happen when life is so overwhelming that you don't know what to do, you might collapse or shut down. You stop. You try to numb out. Those are the places where you don't want to get out of bed. You want to stay under your comforter—hibernate away from other people.

I'm thinking about Len who had great stories to tell. At the same time, though, he was a worrier. As we were exploring where he was in his window of tolerance, he became aware of how he uses worry to generate some feeling. It became clear to him that when he feels numb and shut down, his pattern is to cycle into worrying. The more he studied his process he had a big "Ah ha!" moment. He realized that the worrying was his way of trying to get out of the numb state. Worrying generated a little bit of energy, which pushed him out of the numb depression.

One of my coaching clients, Saralee, realized that "I have an unfortunate mechanism that I'm using to calm down anxiety which brings me to numbness. In other words, if I'm anxious, I find myself craving food, sugar, and snacks. Then I eat until I've worked myself to numbness. I finally realized I've traded anxiety for the unpleasant body sensation of too much fullness, of bloatedness, you know, so I would say that sometimes the mechanism for calming hyper-arousal leads directly to numbness. I've been trying to shut down whatever stress I'm in, but then I end up feeling bad physically, and angry at myself for doing this again."

Saralee realized her level of anxiety was so high and she felt so jangled it was hard to find a balance. As many people do, we swing to the other end and get numb. When I led her through a meditation, Saralee had another insight, "Well, I think for me, and I realized this in the beginning of that meditation . . . you know when you asked me to focus on body sensation? I got an insight from my childhood that being sick was safe. It was an area of "protectedness." My mother was capable of caring for me when I was sick, but this notion of her intervening in abuse was more than she could even allow to become an awareness in her consciousness. So, I think in my mind I began to sublimate agitation, anxiety, fear, all the things that were aroused from being involved in an incestuous relationship, and went to bodily sensation because that was . . . within the safe confines and then in dealing with the abuse, I disassociated."

As we connect to our inner experience, we also find that good feelings—good experiences—can be triggering. For example, when Nancy met her husband, someone she felt very safe with, she found herself triggered. Nancy had this awareness, "I find myself at the low end, and at the low end for many, many years and diagnosed with trauma, my trigger was meeting my husband because I told him that I felt so safe with him and I could be me for the first time. And I didn't know at that time what I was saying, but it was enough to send me spiraling down into the really low scale of this. I would totally shut down. I couldn't stand light. I couldn't stand noise. I couldn't speak properly. And I was in bed for two years. I was right down at the bottom. But I now see that as a part of me and it's now like a signal to be aware that I'm either doing too much or I'm not paying attention to what's going on inside. But as soon as I feel like I'm having one of those days, I use that to signal to me to sit down and tune in and find out what's going on. So now I'm grateful for it."

Anything that takes us out of our comfort zone can trigger something. That's normal. Our comfort zone, which we'll look at in the next chapter, is safe and comfortable for a reason! When we step outside of what's been so familiar, our body will set off signals of alarm. Our task is to pause and notice. Are we on the edge of our window of tolerance . . . or way, way out of it?

The skill in this chapter is designed to help you become comfortable as you navigate stepping out of your comfort zone. Before we get to that skill, though, let's take a moment for reflection.

ACKNOWLEDGING YOUR FEELINGS REFLECTION

Now's your time to pause and do some journaling.

What is your way of calming yourself when you're hyper-aroused?

_____
_____
_____
_____
_____

You may have ways that you feel nourish you, and if you're like so many of us, you have ways that are not as healthy as you would like. Take a moment and reflect back on the last time you were over-stimulated. What did you do to quiet yourself?

_____
_____
_____
_____
_____

When you're shut down, what do you do to give yourself a little bit of energy? (Perhaps your way is to turn to caffeine, chocolate, or other stimulants as ways to gather a little bit of energy.) Reflect on the times you were shut down, numb, or depressed. We all have old habitual ways of managing. What's your way?

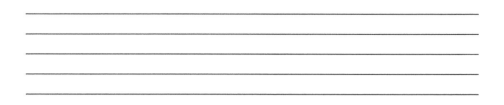

**

What we're trying to do as we work with our window of tolerance is find our way to the edge, while at the same time not being so far out of range—out of our window, that we have to flip to the other side to get back into balance. By working on the edge, we can gently stretch and open, expanding the window so we can tolerate a little bit more over time.

One of the simplest, most eye-opening skills happens when we separate facts from the feelings and interpretations we have about those facts. This essential skill helps rearrange an inner chaotic framework.

This continues to build on what you've been learning so far. Once you can differentiate between a sensation, a feeling, and a thought, you can further explore the difference between what is happening and what is perceived; what is present and what is past.

This is a concept I was introduced to during my years of training with Yvonne Agazarian, PhD, in her Systems Centered Therapy model. It's a helpful skill in making inner space, which I adapted to help people de-escalate their inner experience when feeling triggered. We do that by separating current reality from intrusive reality.

EXERCISE: FACTS, FEELINGS, & INTERPRETATIONS

Gather up a pen/pencil and paper for this next exercise. It's easier to do on paper than a computer, although if you have a tablet that you can draw on, you can try that. Grab something to scribble on. We're not trying to create something polished here; we're just going to play with some ideas a little bit.

I'm going to give you 100 percent permission to not do this right or wrong. How's that for instructions? Our tendency to try to do things right, and not wrong, is so strong that it can actually interfere with learning. I've found, over the years of using this exercise with people, that our tendency is to try to figure out how to do it in our head and miss out on the fun and self-discovery of it. Insight, however, can come much easier when we're not setting the exercise up to avoid doing it wrong.

Here's what we're going to do. I want you to think of a recent experience where you were moderately activated. By that, I mean being around a five on a scale from zero to ten. Maybe a four or a six. You want to choose a memory where you were a little bit activated without being overwhelmed. Being on the edge can work if it doesn't throw you off. This is not a time to be dealing with big triggers, or spiraling into the deepest, darkest pit, or into a huge panic attack. It's important to have a memory associated with some activation, but you must be in a place where you can watch that activation without spiraling. Think of it as being on the edge of your window of tolerance, but not much outside of it.

Step 1: Take a few minutes and write down the experience as it happened. Write it exactly as you were experiencing. As if you were telling your best friend, loaded with all the color commentary, all the feelings, all the thoughts, all the judgment and experience. Just load it all in there and don't try to do this right. Feel free to put some music on that helps you connect with yourself.

Here's an example: If you're reporting a story where you felt furious, write down the whole diatribe. If you were stuttering from anger, add in all the ways you were stuttering. If you felt foolish and you were repeating yourself a thousand times, add all that in. Don't try to clean up the story. Nobody's going to see it! This is just for you. I want you to just write it down the way that it happened in its full glory.

Notice if you're trying to clean up the story, edit it, or censor what you're saying. For this exercise, give yourself full permission to write it as it is. You'll learn more being as authentic as you can be. Got that? Okay.

Step 2: I want you to take a moment to notice your experience. How does your body feel? Take note. What are the sensations in your body right now? Maybe jot that down to remember. As you write this full-spectrum experience down, what happens in your body?

And then following up with what we talked about last time, what thoughts are going on? What feelings are there? Get a sense of what that was all about.

If you were to think of your window of tolerance, are you out of your window? Does it feel tolerable? Are you just at the edge of it? Are you numbed out and shut down? If you're outside your window and unable to follow along with the exercise, perhaps choose another less-activating memory.

Step 3: Ready for the next step? I want you to go through your story. I want you to go through what you wrote down and circle all the **facts** from this experience. Facts, for the purpose of this exercise, are the bare observable facts, and do not include your thoughts or feelings about what is happening (read ahead through Step 4 and Step 5 if you still need more clarity about what a "fact" is here). Once you identify the facts, the next step is to underline the feelings and interpretations from that experience. Simple, right? Circle the facts. Underline the feelings and interpretations.

Step 4: Now, read the story to yourself with just the facts that you circled. Here's a little prompt, "The facts are . . . (and read just the circled words)." Do that about five times. Then notice. What happens in your body? What's your experience when you simply read the facts without anything else?

One of the things you may notice is that we are pretty sneaky people! It's hard to be with the very bare experiences. This goes back to what we learned about mindfulness and bare noticing. We are so used to having charged experiences in our bodies that we load the charge onto the bare facts without even noticing. For example, when Bill did this, he insisted it was a "fact" that he was angry. Let's think about this together. Yes, he was having the felt experience of anger, so in that sense it was a fact. But for our purposes, we want to stay with the observable bare facts— not our interpretations and feelings related to those facts. In Bill's case, he had been at the dentist (who was running late). Bill had rushed to get there, sandwiching this appointment in before picking up his child afterwards, so he was getting anxious, waiting . . . waiting.

As you read this, notice what's happening in your body. Are you aware of any charge, however slight? Certainly, I was aware of the stirring of vicarious anxiety in my own body as Bill and I worked through the issue. So, I wondered with Bill; what would happen if we allowed the facts to be even more bare? I repeated the facts to Bill, "You had a dentist's appointment. The dentist was late. You had to pick up your child." Bill nodded. Yes, those were the facts. After repeating them a few times, I asked him, "What's happening in your body now?" He laughed. Not much. The facts, simple, bare, were boring. There was no charge—which does NOT invalidate the feelings we have about those facts.

Step 5: After you read the facts, add in the following, "The feelings I have about those facts are . . . " continuing with what you have underlined. Do that a few times and then see what is happening in your body.

Robin noticed that as she separated out the facts and feelings, her mind and body slowed down, as did the tension. She reported breathing more easily and her thinking becoming clearer. "When I read just the facts, it felt okay. When I added in the feelings, that activation jumped back in. Gosh, does this help me see how much I hijack what happens!"

Missy laughed realizing how shocking it was. "I was shocked at how strong my reactions were to something that had no reason to be such a problem—it was just a distraction. My interpretations made it personal, intentional, and unreasonably angry. Getting this was really helpful."

Simply said . . .

- Facts are observable data that come through our senses—colors, shapes, sounds, behaviors, tastes, actual observed events, words that were said, body movements, etc.
- Feelings are often the result of unconscious internal commentary on, or the rearrangement of facts. They can enrich and enliven the bare facts of a situation. They can also skew the truth by diminishing it, expanding it out of proportion, or just plain altering it (based on the past).
- If someone has a trauma history, feelings—even good ones—may quickly take someone beyond their window of tolerance. That is, the brain chemistry may instinctively activate trauma responses.

Other examples to clarify these points:

Situation #1 (preparing to teach a BSE workshop):

Facts: I'm typing a handout on my home computer. I sense my fingers clicking on the keys. Next to the computer I have a light switched on that illuminates the pages I printed earlier in the day. I haven't finished designing the session. I see numbers; the clock is telling me the time. My back feels sore; I feel some tension between my shoulder blades. I have the thought that I usually go to bed about this time.

Feelings/Interpretations: I feel excited as I think about who will be at the workshop. As I remember clients who have used this material and how much it's helped them, my heart opens, and I feel glad. I worry a little about finishing on time and getting to bed. I don't want to be tired tomorrow. I feel impatient after a long day.

If I were to stay with the feelings/interpretations, I might have wound myself into feeling worried or pressured to get things done. As I stay with the facts, the worry about the time and fear of being tired doesn't push so much at me. I can focus on the task at hand, enjoy the pleasure of remembering clients who've benefited from the material, and complete the work with ease.

Situation #2 (working with a client):

Facts: A client is sitting in my office. There's a loud noise outside the room. The client notices a man outside the window. The client is startled and can't relax again. Her eyes glaze over and she appears to freeze.

Intervention: I ask my client what happened, facts first. If she's frozen, I might start listing them. If she feels ready, I have her say them.

Recounting Facts: It's helpful if I recount the facts for my client. "There was a loud noise outside. At the same time the noise occurred, you saw a man through the window."

Gently but firmly repeat all the facts, as many times as necessary until the client starts nodding, the body relaxes, and the eyes are alert.

Feelings/Interpretations: "Given that those facts happened outside of you, your response suggests that something happened in your body. (Client nods). You had sensations. (I might repeat the facts if my client starts glazing over or tensing up.) I'm guessing you might have felt numb, tense, or rigid. Is that right? Can you name any other sensations or feelings?"

Most of us jump directly to escalating feelings (based on a rote interpretation of those sensations). "I was scared. I felt something terrible was going to happen. My heart was racing, and I imagined the man was going to reach into this office and get me."

If discussing feelings activates you, stop and go back over the facts. Continue repeating them in a calm and reassuring voice until you feel grounded again. At that point you can guide yourself to begin naming sensations once again.

SEPARATING FACTS FROM FEELINGS REFLECTION

Take a moment to jot down a few thoughts in response to the following questions.

There are times when we are activated, or so full of experience, that we don't want to live inside ourselves or be in touch with what is going on. It's as if we are being battered by a hurricane such that our internal experience feels overcharged. Simply put, we feel out of control.

The storm that embroils us when we're triggered usually consists of more than one component. Each component is probably manageable by itself, but when multiple factors are all jammed together, nothing feels manageable. A simple way to pull apart the myriad components of internal disarray is to organize your inner experience. Recall that we talked about the benefit of using our thoughts to increase our capacity to observe. This experience is designed to help you organize the turmoil and generate enough context to let you move past previous limitations. Once you have sorted out what's happening internally, it becomes easier to target your next step. And those steps are things we will talk about in the coming sections.

Retell the story: Facts first, feelings and interpretations second.

"The facts are . . ."

_____

_____

_____

_____

_____

How do you feel about those facts? Now direct your awareness toward how those facts have influenced you and become aware of your habitual response. One of two things is likely to happen. If you tend to become overwhelmed by feelings, doing this exercise and remembering to breathe should help contain what is happening internally, allowing you to label those feelings/sensations. Conversely, if you tend to go numb, then the experience invites you to let the feelings emerge in a safe way. Let's see what happens for you.

"I feel _____," and/or *"That means _____,"*

_____

_____

_____

_____

_____

If you are overwhelmed, try just repeating the facts in a steady voice, if possible, until you feel more grounded. *"The facts are _____,"* and breathe. *"The facts are_____,"* and breathe. Avoid going into the feelings (i.e., embellishments related to interpretation). Always return yourself to naming facts anytime you catch yourself latching on to feeling or interpreting your experience. Then slowly invite in a reflection on any sensations.

SKILL 5: ADDRESSING PARALLEL LIVES

Objectives:
- To separate past from present
- To explore ways to actively resolve triggers
- To return control to the brain's frontal lobes by knowing when felt experience is out of proportion to what is happening

One of the most painful life experiences for trauma survivors is to be triggered—to go from living in your body, in this present moment, to suddenly finding yourself overcome by fear, terror, numbness, or panic. What, just a moment ago, felt like steady ground now feels enormously disruptive. It often seems as if you're being thrown into another life.

Learning about Parallel Lives offers us another tool to explore and map out our internal territory. We are all less prone to being ambushed by primitive emotions related to the past when we begin to safely explore our emotional landscape. Distinguishing between past and present is key.

Dissociation Barrier

To deal with horrific experiences, the mind has an ingenious means of survival: It compartmentalizes. It takes horrible experience, cordons it off, and puts it behind a formidable barrier—thus keeping the disruptive material at bay. We call this the dissociation barrier. This defense either tones down the affective experience of the event, making it seem more remote and less threatening, or the event is pushed out of conscious memory altogether.

For many people, the barrier eventually becomes more permeable and material gradually leaks through in the form of traumatic symptoms. For others, the barrier is breached more abruptly, and the person may be totally unaware of what created the breach. This helps explain why someone doing seemingly well, enjoying life, and showing no overt signs of trauma, is suddenly assailed by flashbacks, intrusive memories, nightmares, and disturbing body sensations.

Working with the concept of Parallel Lives helps sort out:
1. What is happening in this moment?
2. What undigested material from the past is presenting itself?

Undigested Material and Resolving Triggers

The key point is this: If the experience feels unmanageable and overwhelming, or if we have the impulse to shut it out, triggered material from the past is almost surely involved. By using the Parallel Lives model, you can "re-land" in the present, and use your curiosity to safely explore how past experiences are exploding or intruding into the present. When any of us start to create a link to the origin story of what's triggering us, we start to make sense of what's happening in the present. Our nervous system releases a big sigh.

The process involves learning how to thinly slice history, to find out what happened in a recalled experience, and when it happened. Learning to review a frame-by-frame replay of the experience, and doing so safely within your window of tolerance, gives access to which thoughts, feelings, and sensations happened in each moment, and how those sensations relate to each other.

A big clue is when the experience feels "too big" for the current situation. Continue to learn to slow down the experience so you can "see" into what happened in the frame-by-frame playback. Start by settling into your current experience. Perhaps taking a moment or two to breathe—feel your body in this space. State the bare facts of your current experience . . . are you sitting, standing, walking? What is around you . . . again, just bare naming and noticing . . . a brown chair, etc.

The next step is to either write out or review in your mind what happened and clarify for yourself what the sensations were, what the thoughts were, and what the feelings were.

This may take time, and it's important to take the time. You're looking for the point where the body shifts—going from being in the window of tolerance, to a feeling of overwhelm or numbness. That's the point that needs further investigation and insight.

It's helpful to think of these time capsules as memory fragments. They literally show us a "road map" of how you survived your life. The kinds of automatic thoughts like, "This is so stupid," or "How dare I try to help myself!" or "I've been over this before," we can assume are indicators of the past experience. They could be fragments of encoded experience "describing" your strategy to deal with a terrible situation.

These historical memory fragments are communicated through thoughts, feelings, body sensations, and impulses. They inform us in felt experience how you were impacted. It's often not linear, but rather the internal felt experience being expressed.

When the past is in the past, we can recall material, using our memories to describe or tell a story. Taking some scientific license, I describe these encoded memories as time capsules of experience, filled with thoughts, feelings, and memories. These memories are encoded in various parts of the brain. I have found, however, that using this example helps people understand this concept more easily.

When life is good, we live in the here and now, and move through our lives with greater ease. We're better able to encounter life's ups and downs when we live within our window of tolerance; this helps us integrate our experience. Our dissociative barrier keeps the past in the past and contains these time capsules. For many, this is an adaptive way to live and some energy can be expended, either consciously or unconsciously, to keep the past in the past. For some, however, the dissociative barrier can get breached by an event, such as the birth of a baby, turning a certain age, getting fired, getting married, etc. People's lives are disrupted when such an occurrence precipitates a breach in the dissociative barrier, or if cordoned-off material leaks through into our present. Practicing these techniques can help you discover how to deconstruct these triggers when they occur.

I was recently with some people on a trip overseas. Great trip. Wonderful adventures. Then one day, one of the people—a friend of mine—reached for her wallet and it wasn't there. That meant all her credit cards, passport, everything was gone. In seconds, my friend was sobbing on the street, horrified, distressed. Having known this person for many years, I hugged her and in a firm, calm voice said, "Stay here with us. Nothing bad is happening right here with us!"

I could see she was going down memory lane.

In her mind she was somewhere else in some other time—not here with us, on this street, in this country. At the same time, other people were saying, "She needs to have her feelings!" But I knew there were feelings in the here and now and there were feelings bound up with memories, associations, and feelings states from the past. I knew that if she kept spinning in this emotional distress, she would be catapulted into the past time capsules, continuing to carve an unhelpful pattern deeper into her nervous system, making this old way of being even more emotionally concrete.

We call this a re-enactment. Re-enactments are states that feel like trances as they take over reality. They're reactive states that are usually out of proportion to the circumstances. In their affective bigness they actually give us a doorway into non-narrative patterns that were laid down earlier in life. We all are molded by previous experiences and attachments. However, that early pattern that was laid down is the lens through which we experience and perceive the world. Learning to remap those fundamental patterns is how we break free of the core beliefs in which we feel stuck, hopeless, and despairing.

All that was in my mind as I was with my friend on the street in a foreign country. I knew if she got lost in this physiological distress it would take a lot longer to drain out of her body. So, I stayed right there with her, using a calm voice, getting her to look around her, look at me, look at our friends to see that here in this moment—in this reality—nothing bad was happening. She was here, with people who would take care of her, provide for her, and make sure she was safe physically, financially, emotionally.

In other words, in this moment, nothing bad was happening. As she went through this, she realized that at other times in her past (when the template was being formed) she wasn't allowed to make mistakes, nor were others around her allowed to do things imperfectly. There were always consequences—all of a painful variety.

She learned to adapt, developing strategies to deal with this. But the past fear also stayed buried in her nervous system. When mistakes happen now, the switch opens up a cavern in her mind and out comes this horrifying distress that she's going to be all alone, ashamed, abandoned.

Our task, with ourselves or if helping someone else, is to stay in this moment—this very moment—and to check out reality, creating a distinction between this moment and the past moments that are trying to come to the surface.

The good thing is: Those challenging moments provide us an opportunity to do (to be in) the situation in a different way. The hard thing is: It requires our minds and bodies to not be hijacked by the emotional distress. We need to keep one toe in the upcoming distress, while at the same time hold onto our capacity to witness, observe, and stay present.

Back on the street, we watched our friend's body ease out of its tense hold as she left the "memorized" state of pain that still lived in her body. In this wretched encapsulated state, her felt experience was that life comes out of the blue, hurts you, and you have no recourse to do anything.

Then we did the practical things like contacting credit card companies, etc. After that, we got a little settled and headed back out into the Grand Adventure of Life.

And . . . as life can be . . . a few hours later, my friend reaches into another pocket of her purse and . . . yes . . . discovers her wallet. Right there, where it was all the time. Yet at the moment of emotional escalation (which is what happens to all of us) she was convinced, convinced, convinced that it was taken or lost. She was so convincing that others of us didn't push to look in other pockets. We were convinced with her.

I don't suppose any of you have ever had anything like this happen to you?

Well, the truth is: We all cycle in and out of these kinds of moments. As I said, in psychological terms, we call them "re-enactments." Freud called this a compulsion to repeat. Re-enactments can be torturous when we are caught in the penetrating, usually unconscious, rhythms they hold us in. As a therapist, much of what I do is to enter into re-enactments, willingly and unwillingly with people . . . though trying to help my clients do this consciously instead of unconsciously . . . and in the process of it, shift the outcome.

Much of the healing journey is to discover the range and cycle of the patterns we learned, often non-narratively, from our early environment. We watch how these patterns show up over and over again in many different arenas (ways you might withdraw or react; people you are in relationship with; when you get defensive; on and on). We are looking for clues to this million-piece puzzle, trying to make the experience granular so we can get at it—get our cortex back online, so integration can happen.

These moments, when integrated, prepare us for when life goes BOOM! The old pattern comes right up and shocks us into interacting in old (and usually not the healthiest) ways. We often react in ways we're later embarrassed of, ashamed of, or horrified by.

Despite this, there is good news. We can shift these deeply held patterns by first becoming aware of how they show up in all their permutations, increasing our capacity to be with them without responding in the same old way, and allowing whatever feelings are encapsulated within the pattern. Then, as pieces click into insight and awareness, we are better able to shift.

And that's the whole purpose of this chapter.

> Clara described an experience of feeling enraged, like her head was going to explode. This feeling stemmed from her inability, in that moment, to send an email asking for support. Her turmoil was triggered when her yearning to connect was thwarted, leaving her feeling locked out and left behind. Although flooded with emotion and body sensation, she was able to stay with the facts. She ended up receiving an email and felt a wave of relief from having established a connection.

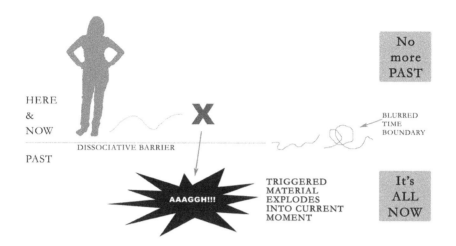

HERE & NOW

PAST

DISSOCIATIVE BARRIER

X

No more PAST

BLURRED TIME BOUNDARY

AAAGGH!!!

TRIGGERED MATERIAL EXPLODES INTO CURRENT MOMENT

It's ALL NOW

Gabriella, a client of mine, spent years working with these concepts in dealing with her frequent triggers. Over time, she realized how the past was leaking into the present. By integrating the past with the present, her body calmed.

One morning, Gabriella explained, she had discovered a leak in the bathroom. In the "here and now" of that moment, she recalled knowing a plumber who previously had done work for her. She knew she could call the plumber, even though the job wouldn't be cheap. Yet, as aware as she was of the facts, her body tensed up, and her mind was consumed with excess nervousness, anxiety, and worry.

After years of practice, Gabriella knew her body was having a reaction that was out of proportion to the event. She collected herself, sat down, and reflected on what was familiar about this situation. A memory floated up. While growing up, her parents over-reacted whenever anything in the house went wrong. Her parents' behavior was so traumatizing that once, when she heard a water pipe bursting in the wall, she wouldn't tell them for fear of being blamed. Although the memory was hard to re-experience, Gabriella was amazed at how much quieter her body felt after a few minutes of exploring the experience and separating the past from the present. Once Gabriella had brought her body back into equilibrium, she called the plumber and made an appointment to have the problem fixed.

How do you know when you're living in the past?

When working with people, I ask them to explain how they know they're in the present moment and to describe the characteristics of being in the past.

When people describe the **present moment**, they usually use words such as: centered, able to concentrate, grounded (can feel my body), mind clear (can concentrate and focus), feel myself here, feel safe with things as they are, things feel right-sized, able to tolerate shades of grey, can feel my feelings (good, bad, in between), connected inside and out, things roll off my back, there's a sense of spaciousness, aware of my inside being different than what's happening outside.

To describe the feelings of being in the **past,** they often use: worried, needing to obsess, hopeless, despairing, terrified, numb, blank, depressed, exhausted, paralyzed, caught in black and white thinking, flooded, trying to survive, hyper-vigilant, performing ritualized behaviors, feeling on the verge of acting out, powerless.

If you're lucky to be able to talk with safe others, knowing how people describe what happens when undigested material arises can help you normalize these sometimes shame-filled responses. Remember that all reactions (anything that feels too big, out of proportion to the moment, or outside the window of tolerance) is likely triggered by something from the past.

Example: Working with Andy

A male client, Andy, was at a party and got triggered. In our session, he told me he was angry with himself for not being in control and behaving inappropriately. He was surprised at the amount of anger he felt for "no reason." (BIG CLUE—the amount of anger surprised him, and he felt there was no apparent reason.)

I suggested that we "notice every little thing," and pointed out to him that he had somehow been triggered. I asked him what he remembered and where we should start. Andy remembered seeing a friend talking to a stranger at the party.

I asked him what T/F/S (again, this stands for thoughts/feelings/sensations) he was having at that time. He responded that he felt okay—not having the best time *(emotional experience)*. He added, they both seemed to know each other *(thought)*. "I was an outsider" *(another thought)*. He continued, "I didn't like feeling like I was becoming wallpaper" *(more emotional experience and a visual image)*.

I wanted him to share more of this experience with me, so I asked, "What created the sense of wallpaper?" Andy responded that he felt people at a party should circulate, but this group just "clotted up." He explained, "I felt left out *(feeling)* and couldn't think of anything to say. I didn't want to butt into a conversation *(feeling and thought)*, so I walked to the bathroom to sober up and wash my face *(events)*.

When I came out and looked around, I decided I didn't like those people. I didn't have to be there. That's when I got irritated and angry" *(feeling)*.

I was still trying to find out more about the experience, since there wasn't an obvious link to the past. So, I asked him, "Was there something about being wallpaper?" Andy responded, "I really wanted them to like me. But then I didn't care if they liked me either."

I prompted him by asking if there was anything familiar about that experience of wanting someone to like you, but then not caring if they did. Andy replied, "If I can't control the situation, I'd rather not be a part of it." (Controlling often means someone is not within their window of tolerance and must do something to feel safe.)

I wondered out loud with him where he learned to need to have that kind of control, where he hated being ignored, and where he needed to be one up on people. With that, it clicked, and he told me about a part of his history—when his younger brother would get out of control. It was better for Andy when he didn't fight back. If he stayed calm, he didn't "get killed" by his brother, and his parents didn't blame him or get mad at him instead of his brother.

Andy felt sad as he remembered this period in his life. Since our time together was short for processing either the anger or the sadness, we mapped out his internal territory. We learned that Andy is extremely afraid of his anger and has been prone to depression.

We drew out the Parallel Life of this event: By always shutting off his anger when his brother was out of control, Andy ended up pushing those emotions into a time capsule of sorts that kept him safe in those moments of perceived danger. The time capsule treatment also served to ward off his sadness at being ignored by his parents when he was scared. Focused on his brother, his parents were unable to comfort Andy.

By uncovering that historical piece, we were then able to see more clearly how he might get triggered in situations where he feels ignored and extraneous. Andy's body softened some, even as he acknowledged that he did not want to be in that kind of dilemma again. Together we set out to outline some strategies for dealing with those triggers in case they resurfaced.

Once you know the T/F/S of a situation, you have the option to stay in the present and explore another possible, more satisfying path. And that is a skill we'll cover in the section "Carving Out a New Path."

Take a moment to jot down a few thoughts in response to the following questions. At some point, be sure to take time to explore these questions further. They don't have to be done all at once. Some of them may take more time to answer than others. If you feel comfortable, talk to your friends or your therapist about the questions. Reach out to others and find out what works for them too.

If you have a trauma history, you know the experience of having been triggered into your history—into painful, dark, and overwhelming spaces. That's an unfortunate given. People wish they could shut this stuff off—keep it away—however, most are unsuccessful in doing so. With practice, you eventually learn to befriend the overwhelming material in small bites and learn to neutralize the charge. Using the Becoming Safely Embodied skills can give you the tools to help you deconstruct your triggers when you're on your own. When you're with your therapist, you can access more of your painful history as you're ready.

Always take a moment to land in the present moment if you can. Being present is a term that describes the experience of being curious, open, and interested in this moment, right here and now. When you're present, you can identify what's going on in your inner landscape, and you feel as if you have some control over what's happening. At those times, life feels in proportion without feeling overwhelming.

In this moment, how do you become aware you're here in this body, at this time? How do you know whether you are in the past or in the present? Take a moment to access that experience in your body. If it helps, write it down or make a drawing of the felt experience.

What helps you live more in the here and now?

_____

_____

_____

_____

_____

Getting triggered happens when some unfinished piece of your history gets activated in your current moment. You might feel overwhelmed or go numb, feel spaced out, life might feel too big or you may feel like you're trapped inside a storm. At those times you can assume you are dealing with triggered experiences from the past. What happens in your body, mind, and heart when you're triggered?

_____

_____

_____

_____

_____

What situations, for you, tend to trigger the past exploding into the present?

_____

_____

_____

_____

_____

How might the past be intruding in your present here and now moment? Something from the past is coloring or distorting your present experience in some way. These triggers can take the form of kinesthetic, auditory, and visual memories, as well as flashbacks and trance states. Even though these are memories, they're not necessarily experienced that way. In fact, they may feel as though they're happening again in the present. Learning to recognize that these are undigested memories can help you become freer in the here and now.

_____

_____

_____

_____

_____

What helps you become aware of how the past colors your present?

_____

_____

_____

_____

_____

How might you practice these techniques so they become resources that you could use when needed?

_____

_____

_____

_____

_____

What skills do you know that might help? (Facts/feelings work? Belongingness techniques? *Metta*? Mindfulness?)

_____

_____

_____

_____

_____

RESOLVING TRIGGERS REFLECTION

1. Create safety for yourself. First things first. If you are in a triggering environment and feel out of control, you might need to leave the situation before you do anything you later regret. That might mean going to a bathroom, to a separate office if you're at work, or going for a walk. Sometimes we need space to decompress. Men often need more time than women to lower their physiological arousal. If possible, take whatever time you need. That might mean telling the person you are with that you will be right back, or back in ten to twenty minutes. If the situation is unsafe, you don't have to be graceful, thoughtful, or even considerate in leaving. What's most important is that you feel safe. As you practice these skills, you'll find you can stay in the situation and keep working on yourself without anyone noticing your effort.

    If you're in a situation where you must be present or appear to be present and are still struggling with the triggering material, take a moment for some self-talk. It is sometimes helpful to tell these activated parts that you really want to hear what happened and why they got so triggered, but right now you can't be present to them in the way you would like. At those times, it's good to let your parts know that you will spend time with them. Set a time and keep that promise!

    If you can stay in the situation without increasing the stress to intolerable levels, then explore what else you might need to increase the sense of safety. Do you need to call someone? Talk to a trusted person who is nearby? Take out a piece of paper and write? Talk to yourself? Touch something soft? Or something solid? Grab a special stone you carry?

2. Explore what happened. When you are feeling more stable, perhaps removed from where you felt triggered or in a quiet space, you could explore what happened. For some, this means waiting until you are at your therapist's office. For others, it may be in another safe space. Once you notice where the past is intruding, your chances of deconstructing it increase.

3. Deconstructing the triggers: Take stock of every detail that happened. Sometimes seemingly meaningless things create the trigger, but we overlook them. We're looking for things in the present which look/feel/smell/sound like something from the past.

   Start your review from the "before" point. Where were you before you got triggered? What were you thinking, feeling, and what was going on in your body? Take your time and be discerning. Then take the next slice of time. Think of a storyboard from an animation or a movie—they go frame by frame. That's what we're doing here. Start your exploration of what happened with that first frame. Walk your way through time until the "big bang." What happened? What T/F/S (thoughts/feelings/sensations) were going on? Is there anything familiar about those T/F/S? A key to deconstructing the triggers is to notice what was familiar about the experience, what pulls you to the past—both internally and externally.

   At some point, a memory or association will arise, often spontaneously. For some, having that association "click into place" allows them to relax. That may not always be the case for everyone. Whatever happens, though, it's a good idea to write down the association. Many people keep a notebook on hand to jot down the facts of the situation. Then, notice the feelings you had—without going into them. Note them on paper (like you did in the Bare Attention Exercise) and process them with your therapist or other safe/wiser person.

Carol: "I do understand the difficulty in trusting our body and many people's experience, including my own. The body has almost become an enemy."

Deirdre: "So, how about taking it very slowly? With little steps at first. Even a tiny fraction of a moment. This is so powerful. Listening to other people in how they're teaching us out of their own experiences can help everyone learn."

Carol continues: "The overarching lesson I learned from the BSE is the importance of going slowly. When I'm pushing too hard, too fast, my body tends to shut down again. In my own life, slowing down helped my body, helped me be able to with it and me with it, if that make sense."

Deirdre added: "Our bodies have done an excellent job in many ways. Underneath those layers our body wants to help get us through. It's all about learning to trust your body."

"I love your teaching, Deirdre, for it has imbued all the vexing thoughts, feelings and sensation signals which infiltrate my present experience in fragmented form with SIGNIFICANCE. Now, instead of grading feelings and sensations as deserving of significance or not, I can give all feelings, all sensations, and all thoughts the significance they deserve, creating a helpful value system."

Fact: I've been having conversations with someone that is bringing up a lot of feelings I didn't expect. And I'm feeling charges from someone I did not expect.

Thoughts: They did something wrong. They wronged me! Something's not right here!!!

Feeling: anger

Sensations: hot inside, system charge is amping up

The pieces: young parts permeating the dissociative barrier to my adult part

Internal sensation: overcharge-ping, ping, ping, fight-flight

Feeling: desperate

Thought: I'll lose. I'll cave.

Sensation: high charge, or high amperage

Thoughts: Watching this, I'm aware that a part of me is supplying a lot of charge, more than my system is carrying comfortably. How is this a carryover from early circumstances that this circumstance has pinged? Hmmm. My uncle terrorizing me. He enjoyed getting a rise out of me.

Feeling: calming, grounded as I see how pieces fit together

Thought: What was overcharging my system is now digestible.

Sensation: release and energy freely circulating

Feeling: empathy with my triggering circumstances' charge, sympathy, sadness, and compassion—especially for myself

Another option is to notice what's familiar when you get triggered. How is this familiar experience a map of how you survived? What are the different components? Can you draw out or describe your beliefs/thoughts, feelings, and sensations?

SKILL 6: WORKING WITH PARTS

Objectives:
- To learn (or review) some basic psychology and neurobiology to set the stage
- To practice staying centered even in charged situations
- To identify triggers as triggers
- To keep reinforcing that you are more than your activation
- To learn to become experimental. Try things out. Becoming curious about what happens and why it happens. What happens if you change things slightly? You can always ask yourself: Did I end up feeling better, worse, or the same?

Survivors benefit tremendously from becoming more aware of what happens when we're triggered. But being triggered is still distressing, and that distress can easily engulf us in chaos, especially when we first start practicing new ways. We need simple skills to calm, soothe, and reassure internal psychological states to dare to be more present and more aware.

There are many psychological approaches for interacting with internal states (parts) that have been developed, including Gestalt Therapy (Perls) and Psychosynthesis, the work of Roberto Assagioli, Ego State Therapy (Watkins & Watkins, 1997), the Structural Dissociation Model (van der Hart, Nijenhuis, Steele, 2006), Internal Family Systems (Schwartz, 1997), and the work of Compassion Focused Therapy developed by Paul Gilbert and his colleagues around the world.

Compassion Focused Therapy (CFT) uses "chair work"—a derivative of Gestalt therapy—where people externalize their internal state/part, moving into a different chair and "becoming" that part as a way to learn more about that part. A chair is set up for the Compassionate Self who is there to help the person be with the experience from a compassionate perspective.

Richard Schwartz, who developed Internal Family Systems, describes three main groups: the "exile" who had to be dissociated out of the system to survive, the "firefighter" who tends to wreak havoc in an attempt to protect these "exiles," and the "manager" who manages the system. The IFS model includes an additional component—the "Self"—that part in each of us that holds limitless qualities of compassion, curiosity, clarity, courage, and confidence.

Gestalt techniques frame these portions of the self as disowned aspects of self that can be reintegrated.

The Structural Dissociation Model adapted Charles Meyers' work observing World War II veterans to develop their model of the Apparently Normal Part of the Personality (ANP) and the various parts of the personality that are holding the emotional trauma (EPs).

Peter Levine's (1997) approach was informed by watching studies and film of animals in their native habitat and focusing on "animal defenses." He then applied his findings to human beings in terms of the basic responses we make in the face of danger. Our first response is to **fight**. If it's not safe to fight, our bodies initiate the **flight** impulse. In moments when neither of those responses are suitable, our physiological response is to **freeze**. That freeze response is also referred to as "deer in the headlights." Trauma survivors also experience the absence of feeling, or being in a numb state. Clients will describe this state as frozen, but completely activated by anxiety. **Submitting and complying** is the last response an animal will choose. Biologists suggest that most carnivores prefer not to eat dead meat, so if the other animal is feigning death, the hunter may cease attacking.

Janina Fisher's approach integrates our understanding about neurobiological regulation of trauma; we can also use this model to help clients learn to regulate themselves. In the 1950s, Paul MacLean proposed that we don't have just one brain, but three—the Triune Brain Model. Although much of his theory has since been superseded, it's still useful to think of the brain as having a few major parts:

The **brainstem**, at the base of the brain (as the name suggests), is similar in structure to the reptilian brain, and acts as a "relay center" handling many automatic functions. It monitors our basic needs: breathing, fight or flight responses, digestion, and heart rate, among others.

The **cerebellum** is located between the brainstem and the cerebrum, coordinating muscle movements, balance, and guiding posture.

The **cerebrum**, divided into left and right hemispheres, is the largest and most complex of the three, and controls learning, interpreting sensory data, emotions, and fine control of movement. Humans have a very high brain-weight-to-body-weight ratio AND more neurons per unit volume than other animals. The cerebral hemispheres have discrete fissures, dividing each hemisphere into four lobes. Each hemisphere has four lobes: The frontal plays a key role in reasoning, emotions, judgment, and voluntary movement; the temporal in hearing, smells, and memory; the parietal is critical in touch and spoken language, and the occipital in vision and reading ability.

Located in the middle of the brain is the **limbic system**, crucial to our emotional life and also central to memory, motivation, and behavior. The limbic system includes, though the science is evolving, the amygdala, or the part of the brain that gets activated when danger is sensed, and the hippocampus, which helps processing of memories.

In general, our ability to stay in the present moment is governed by a developed cortex and our traumatic dysregulation is tied closely to limbic activation. Our central nervous system (CNS) has two branches: the sympathetic, which activates us and gets us going, and the parasympathetic, which calms us down after being activated. Training programs like Sensorimotor Psychotherapy are excellent methods in aiding activation/control of the CNS.

When you're using the Becoming Safely Embodied model, you're learning entry-level steps and how to implement those steps outside of therapy. It's helpful to focus on calming, reassuring, and soothing yourself so that you have more "bandwidth" to deal with the complications of life when they arise.

I often think of John Gottman's work with couples. One of the big findings of his research is that for every even slightly negative thing that happens to a person in a couple, they need to have 5 positive things in their "emotional bank account" to buffer the intensity of the one negative thing. When we're healing, we need this as well. The more our body is at ease, the easier it is to be with the trigger.

In this chapter you'll learn to respond, validate, and acknowledge your individual systems, forming the basis for self-regulation. As you open to your inner world, you'll find it necessary to work with the more disenfranchised or exiled parts that resist efforts to being soothed or placated. As many people find it difficult to work with those parts on their own, it's a good time to explore individual therapy.

Parallel Conversations

Megan...

HERE & NOW	Chronological Age	48 years old, former executive, good, solid friends,
	Current Life Situation	

We often have layers of realities inside, going on at the same time. I describe this as having Parallel Conversations that can occur simultaneously. Let me use a composite example with Megan.

Megan, a successful female executive, was referred by her therapist to attend one of my skill-building groups. Megan was "on the fast track," someone her company was grooming to fill positions of higher responsibility.

Triggered by something that occurred at work and unable to focus, Megan sought out her therapist for help. Suddenly, she was starting to struggle and rationalized that she'd always been able to overcome past obstacles; so why not now?

With no training in dissociation, her therapist's approach only intensified her symptoms. Megan's therapist eventually increased her therapy sessions to two to three times per week, each session lasting two to three hours.

This arrangement satisfied Megan's many layers. Some of her parts wanted to be rescued, so they loved the attention. Craving it, they kept wanting more. They regressed. They loved this world where someone was taking care of them, something they had never received before. They could hang on to someone, and they no longer had to push away the needy parts.

That was all happening on just one layer and the conversation at that level was, "Don't leave me!" . . . in other words, the felt experience was, "I got really hurt before when people left me and didn't take care of me, don't leave me now." Another part, however, was feeling neglected and was crying silently in the corner, "Waah!" The felt conversation was: "I need help, come help me. I'm hurting." Yet another part was having an entirely different conversation. That part was yelling, "I hate you!" which was a way to express feeling trapped and scared to death of this person who was so different.

Parts at different levels may be engaged in similar conversations; this can make it difficult for clients to respond to a therapist's question. One question could evoke multiple responses, all demanding attention at the same time. It's important to be able to separate out all those different internal voices/parts so they can be addressed with kindness, understanding, and respect. Sometimes being with one part that's the loudest can send signals of attunement throughout the system.

Cultivating compassion for ourselves is always helpful when we look at our internal states; these are usually areas where we don't feel very confident. Having a compassionate stance while holding the elements of noticing what's going on— dis-identifying, becoming aware, and externalizing—staunches the proliferation of negative self-talk.

Being centered is important. That can happen by asking your internal world to give you some space so you can shift gears, bringing your attention to them with compassion. This may mean taking some time to externalize the various parts, identifying them by simple words or a drawing and playing with them around you, outside your body.

Since we are more than the sum of our parts, getting centered is the first pathway opening us to our own inner wisdom. Remember, perspective is important. If all you're aware of is the triggered part, it will be hard to access other important components of the internal dialogue. By making contact with the Compassionate Self (as with CFT), "Self" (as with IFS), or "wise mind," you'll be able to embody this larger sense of awareness of who you are, instead of being locked into the triggered reality. This perspective accesses our inner wisdom, soul, or higher self, which can guide us through difficulties that arise. If you are struggling to access and embody your Compassionate Self, it might help to think about someone who seems to embody their own internal wisdom. For some, that could be a loved one, safe family member, therapist, spiritual figure, or even television personalities like Oprah. Identifying and naming those qualities you're looking for helps make the idea of compassion more concrete.

By being grounded in your own inner wisdom, you'll be able to make contact with what's going on inside you. As you begin to resonate and open to your inner wisdom, notice the effect that has on your body. Do you feel more present? Does this allow you to have a sense of ease? What do you notice first? For example, is it dead quiet in there, a screaming cacophony, or something else? Are you drawn to the tension in a shoulder muscle, or tightness elsewhere? Perhaps you see images or memories that are filtering into your consciousness?

Remember, there's no right way to do this . . . or wrong way. This is a process of befriending your inner world, welcoming the psychological parts, emotional parts, and sensations that are there. Whatever it is, bring it to your mind's eye and connect with it from this centered observing state. That which observes itself is wise.

You'll then be able to explore and inquire in a more focused way. What might the various parts be trying to communicate to you? Pain? Terror? Anger? Distress? Joy? Happiness? How do they communicate? Through thoughts? Feelings? Sensations? Images? Memories? Blankness?

Notice your responses to these questions. Invite parts to share their responses with you. If you need, take a breath, exhale slowly, and create space within. When you have some space inside notice how you feel toward the part that's clamoring for attention.

Practice responding with self-compassion. This might not be easy at first, because these emerging parts have long felt disowned and unwanted. This is where having a felt experience of compassion is really helpful. When you can access somatic memory of being with compassionate people, it's much easier to flow that compassion toward any part that is triggered.

With openhearted awareness, open yourself to find out more: What does this part need to hear or feel from you? Is it the reassurance that you are willing to listen? Is it to be held? Is it words of comfort? Is it a special song that this part wants you to sing? Take the time you need here. If you find yourself getting overwhelmed or shut down, pause. Acknowledge that this can be hard. Find a way to orient toward what's nurturing and supportive.

Every part of us needs to be validated, seen, known, and cared for, even when they present as scary, grief-stricken, or terrified. It can be helpful to interact with these parts, reminding them that you're learning with them, wanting to make contact, even if you don't always know the best way to do so. Different prompts could be, "Even though you frighten me, I'm wanting to learn how to care for you." "This is new. I'm trying something different. I can go slow and learn along the way." Or

"Hey you guys, could you give me some room here so I can actually be with you? If you overwhelm me, you'll be alone again, and I know that's not what you want."

All along, continue to observe what's happening. What thoughts are there? Feelings? How is your body, your heart responding? With steady attention and interest, notice how this part responds to the communication. Does it flinch? Relax? Cry harder? Staying centered in your Compassionate Self or your adult self will help you draw on every resource to care for and soothe this previously disowned part. You'll notice, as you do this, that you become aware of internal capabilities you didn't know you had; with time and practice, your abilities will grow and true healing can begin.

Remember, this takes time and the re-learning of trust may undergo many challenges followed by small successes. Keep remembering to return to, and trust in that centered, loving, place of wisdom within yourself that holds a greater perspective. Learning to be with ourselves takes patience and compassion, so be gentle with yourself. Offer yourself kindness as you explore the best ways to be with yourself.

Wayne explained to Deirdre that his disowned parts tend to be speaking all at once, and this baffled him. To tease out what the voices were saying, Wayne decided to write everything down. As he paid closer attention, he realized that the voices could be differentiated by age, so he used colored pens to represent the voices. He assigned pink to a young self, green to an angry teenager self, and purple to his wise self.

At first, none of what Wayne wrote down made any sense. The process of listening to those voices and writing down their words, however, helped Wayne manage his experience. Although not everything he wrote was helpful, the practice helped Wayne find themes that he shared with his therapist.

Prior to using colored pens, Wayne characterized his relationship to these parts, as "owning them, but not owning them." Taking the time to know and respect his inner voices allowed Wayne to form a deeper relationship with those disaffected parts. Wayne emphasized that this was a slow process.

Deirdre applauded Wayne's idea of using colored pens and praised Wayne for externalizing his T/F/S. Deirdre then asked Wayne what allowed him to remain persistent. Wayne felt the exercise helped him gain clarity with his inner dialogue. He added that being self-compassionate was essential.

Creating Soothing Self-Talk

You've probably noticed the emphasis I'm making on kindness, gentleness, and compassion. Building this inner world—where it's safe to trust, where it's possible to build a compassionate, kind, and supportive environment—is a core principle of *Becoming Safely Embodied*.

This is certainly something we want to practice when you are "speaking" to yourself. How often are you using kind, generous, open-hearted language? How does that compare to the times you speak negatively to yourself? Notice when it seems to happen; what triggers it? What have become your default ways to diminish yourself?

Becoming aware of how you treat yourself, and in what manner, is the first step. That is, we must practice treating ourselves gently and compassionately. Otherwise, that awareness can be used to increase the hopelessness and suffering.

Once you become aware, over time you'll be inspired to make different choices to achieve more constructive outcomes. No matter what happens, be aware of what transpires. Basically, your goal is to feel better than worse; to be relieved rather than discomforted.

Suggestions for Developing Wholesome Self-Talk

1. Dis-Identifying

There are different ways to dis-identify from something. The main idea is to find a way to take what is going on inside of you and separate from it without dissociating. In this way, we find that our observing self can witness what is happening to another part.

At times, we can dis-identify psychologically by thinking about differences; sometimes activities such as writing, drawing, singing, or moving your body are more helpful. Whatever choice you make, try noticing whether there is a grounded internal observer who is paying attention to what is happening.

Noting: If you are feeling flooded, you may find it helpful to name what's overwhelming you, and then label the emotions—anger, jealousy, or anxiety. As with meditation, the simple act of noticing (noting) can help you externalize the experience, that is, psychologically putting it outside of yourself. By practicing saying *"Anger. Anger. Anger,"* or *"Sadness. Sadness. Sadness,"* you give yourself space to breathe, which helps slow down the feeling of overwhelm.

When we're flooded, we must remember to breathe before we can proceed, and realize that there's more to us than this triggered part. At those times, naming or labeling parts will encourage dis-identification. Simply note that you're feeling triggered. Noting the sensation or feeling helps you slow down, so you can identify and name/label your emotions. In this way, you reduce the impact of the overwhelm.

"I'm really triggered . . . I'm really triggered."

Externalizing: Sometimes noting isn't enough. These internal voices may control sizable psychological real estate. When these parts are at full strength, they often take over with a vengeance. If we're not held captive by them, we might simply recognize them as parts trying to do their "jobs" of protecting us and keeping us safe. In their grasp, we may find ourselves feeling like hostages.

To counteract these parts, notice where in the body the experience is located. They can, at times, even feel as if they're outside of your body. Take a moment to locate the part. This state can show up as thoughts (words in your head), feelings, sensations, or images. Realize that whatever comes up is a communication from that part. Perhaps your chest starts feeling heavy and under pressure. The feeling might increase, or it may cause you pain. That sensation may be the part trying to say something to you—to remind you of the experience it was feeling at some earlier time in your life.

You might notice a sense of a "force field" around your body, or a sense of not being able to move. Sometimes your head gets noisy, as if a kindergarten class at recess rushed in. Some people just notice feeling states, or they have an image of being somewhere at a certain age. Whatever comes up, take note, and use the information as an access point.

"It's in my head. It's so noisy I can't even figure out what the words are."

"My belly feels like there's a sick blob in there. Makes me sick."

"I feel like a pinball machine, everything's bouncing off the walls."

"I want to curl up in a ball and shut everyone out."

Once you have a clearer idea of this triggered part, speak to it as if it's apart from you. That's a simple way of dis-identifying from it, recognizing that there is a part of you inside that is having the experience, and another part of you that is witnessing and observing the triggered part from the outside. It can be helpful to treat these parts as you would a child who is overwrought and needs a time out. Speak to the triggered part as best you can with kindness and confidence.

"You're really triggered, aren't you? I want to know what's happening. I see that you're really distressed (or sad, or angry, or frustrated, or scared, or hurt). It matters to me that you're upset, but I'm afraid I won't do a good job in listening. I'm afraid I might get scared, but I'm willing to try, and if I can't do it well now, I'll try again."

In whatever way you feel comfortable, let these troubled parts know you're open to them, and ready to listen. To feel comfortable may require you to breathe and ground yourself. If so, take your time; slow down so you don't lose yourself in the situation. Take a walk if necessary. Movement can help alleviate potential flooding brought about by the emotional state.

Sometimes we must be more concrete in externalizing these parts. Try drawing the experience, writing it down, or in some way putting it outside of yourself. Develop details of this internal experience. How does the voice sound? Where in your body does this part live? What does this part look like? A blob, a dark cloud, a four-year-old, or a mean prison guard? Once you've externalized the part, make it as true for yourself as it is when it's bound up inside of you.

Then, consciously observe that part through your eyes and senses. Taking this step moves this internalized version of the part outside of you. Feel free to move this part as far away from you as needed to create some safe space.

If you find yourself getting overwhelmed, or slipping back into identifying with the triggered part, ask the parts to slow down and not overwhelm you. Be as kind as possible and as steady as you can.

Take another breath or two to center yourself. Notice your feelings now that this part has been externalized. If you feel no different, you can be sure that the triggered part has slid back into position! Or, there might be another part "protecting" you, to keep you from feeling calmer. Sometimes protector parts do that to make sure you don't get hurt and nothing bad happens.

If you can't get centered, breathe in kindness, compassion, healing light, or whatever energy/feeling feels best to you. Focus on this kindness. Concentrate on it without any pressure. Take your time to savor and soak up this different energy.

We all have parts of ourselves that don't exemplify who we want to be. It helps to compartmentalize the meanness (or other troubling parts) by putting them into a separate compartment. It's another way of separating from them. Deliberately addressing those parts as separate from you may allow for some sense of freedom or safety, and it can help you pay closer attention to them. Some people find it necessary to put these parts in a box, or a container of some kind. Psychologically, this can be done through your imagination, or you may write or draw what the part represents, placing that artifact in a container, and stashing the box somewhere. Some people have even buried the container! Trust yourself and create the psychic space you need to calm down.

2. Learning to Befriend These States

When you notice yourself being triggered by internal noise, it's the perfect time to practice compassion and loving-kindness! It's hard, at first, to see the internal voices as parts of yourself, but with practice, you can externalize the part and begin to intervene compassionately.

Our first instinct when someone is mean or rude to us is to respond in kind. When our parts speak to us in a critical or demeaning way, our usual response is to sink into it, become it, or become compliant. With practice, we can slow ourselves down to create some internal distance, and give ourselves a chance to respond in a more helpful way.

The key to developing this compassion is to realize these parts are just doing tasks that were given to them long ago. With practice, you can begin to see their behavior as messages from the past. Unfortunately, these behaviors transition from internal impulses, thoughts, or feelings into "real life" re-enactments, often showing up as explosive rage, self-destructive behaviors, complete withdrawal, overeating, obsessing, or other forms of extreme behavior. The Internal Family Systems model calls these parts "firefighters." Firefighters will do anything to protect the exiled part from being hurt or exposed again. When this happens, we often find ourselves startled, overwhelmed, or confused.

Once you see their behavior as messages from the past instead of as your being out of control, pay closer attention and befriend them. As you accustom yourself to this new approach, you will begin to enjoy a happier, more compassionate internal experience.

Try linking the internal noise, behavior, or feeling to the past. Imagine that what you are feeling is simply the undigested experience that was encoded long ago. An infant, child, or even young adult, is not yet developed enough to deal with a lot of overwhelm. They don't know what to do with it. People typically push overwhelming material out of their minds, into some cordoned off psychological space, where it no longer intrudes into daily life (review the section on Parallel Lives if needed). What you are feeling now may be the intensity that you were not able to "digest" when you were younger. In this way, your current experience is vital in knowing why the past was so difficult, and is key to creating a more satisfying future.

"Wow. That's intense. If it's this hard for me now, it must have been brutally intolerable for me when I was _____ (fill in the age)."

During this process, check to see whether the part is listening to you or paying attention. If you don't get prompt internal feedback, ask the part if it's aware you are there. Usually there's some answer, otherwise, the part may be hiding, worried, discouraged, or upset. Since we don't know, you might try talking to it as kindly as you can:

> "I know I haven't always been there for you. I want you to know I'm trying to learn how to do this. I know I must do it differently than I've been doing. I make mistakes and don't always know how to talk to you or take time to listen to you. I hope you'll be patient with me. You can always let me know when I'm doing something that isn't working for you."

When you have achieved some internal balance—it needn't be a 100 percent improvement—try speaking kindly to these critical or frantic voices. By practicing kindness, you're creating internal room to witness them more supportively. Then you can welcome these parts as you would welcome a guest to your house. The intention is to befriend these parts, instead of continuing to push them away.

> "I know you're really hurting but beating me up doesn't help me listen any better. Can you tone down the energy so I can be more present and hear what you have to say?"

3. Setting Loving or Kind Boundaries

Sometimes it's too much to try to "process" anything psychologically. You might be feeling stressed or burned out by your own physiology. Be gentle with yourself. This is the perfect time to practice compassion, which could include "dropping the content" and turning your attention elsewhere.

Good concentration is helpful. As you try to shift your attention, the triggered part will still be pulling at you. Increase your focus on where you want to go, rather than what is tugging at you. Many people find practicing *metta* useful in refocusing their energy away from the internal noise without dissociating. Focusing on something new can provide a boundary. You might knit, play an instrument, review multiplication tables, weed your garden, or a million other neutral-to-positive endeavors.

Occasionally, parts are not ready for (or interested in) kindness, care, and compassion. Some parts are so angry or hurt that all they've known how to do is to fight. Just as you set boundaries with others who are cruel or insensitive, you can do the same with yourself. Internal boundaries help to make sense of the chaos you're feeling when life gets too overwhelming.

> "I understand how upset you are. But it's not okay for you to treat me this way."
>
> "If you want my attention, then let's find a way for it to work for both of us."

Time Boundary: As we've already discussed, a part may need to take a time out to calm down. You may find yourself at work when a part gets triggered, but you know you can't deal with that level of emotion at that moment. Let this part know that you can't do anything with it right now, but that you'll find time later to listen. Commit to a specific time when you can revisit the situation with this part. Ensure that you don't promise to listen while you're driving the car, or when other responsibilities demand your attention!

You may need to let this part know that you can't work with it on your own and that you're going to bring this up with your therapist. It may help to call and arrange for an additional session.

Some parts will continue to "fight" for attention. Practice letting the agitated parts know with a firm, loving voice that this is not the time. You can't tend to them right now, but you will return soon. If possible, let them know when, and with whom you'll bring up their concerns.

4. Creating an Antidote

Sometimes when we're in painful situations, we use fantasy or magical thinking to tolerate our upset. Instead, offset the painful, distressing experience with what you want to cultivate in your life.

"I am feeling so much pain. I really want to hurt less. May I be at peace."

"I hate myself. While that feels true right now, I really want to find a way to care about myself."

"I don't want to be present. I want out. And yet, I know there are other parts of me that want to be here.

Self-Soothing Strategies

Be willing to track your experience and monitor your level of upset. In this way, you can begin to intercede and interrupt the upset—before it gets out of control.

Here is a recap of some ideas to help you develop the ability to effectively monitor your internal states and properly intervene:

1. Once you've practiced and learned how to consciously breathe when you're upset, keep practicing. The more often you do this, the more likely your default response will be to breathe with awareness when you are triggered. No matter how upset you are, you can always return to the safety of meditating on your breathing. Several breathing techniques could benefit you. Specifically, you might want to practice the *kumbach* breathing technique: Inhale gently, yet almost fully, and hold your breath for a moment. Slowly exhale, until your lungs are nearly empty. Wait a beat or two without inhaling right away. Then repeat. You may also, with practice, extend the holds longer than a beat or two.

2. It is often helpful to stop talking and to stop thinking about the story; otherwise we find ourselves repeating the same story! Resisting the urge to recite the story will help de-escalate the upset and lower your heart rate. Many people find the exercise of Separating Facts from Feelings to be most helpful at this point.

3. If you haven't been able to slow yourself down while in the presence of what's upsetting you, consciously take some space. If that level of upset and activation happens when interacting with another person, excuse yourself and let them know when you'll return. Ten minutes may suffice, or you may need more time. Regain your equilibrium by disconnecting from the situation. (Note: Remember that taking time out during an upset in a close relationship is not the same as leaving the relationship.)

4. Practice relaxing the muscles that are holding tension by breathing into them. Sometimes people tense their bodies to ward off unpleasant sensations and feelings. They become "armored." Notice if that's true for you. Remind yourself that any kind of inner experience can be befriended. Talk to the feelings that are threatening to overwhelm you. If this were a beloved friend, lover, or child, what would help make it possible for you to befriend their feelings?

5. When you feel anxious, bring your energy down into the body, instead of following the energy out of the body. Feel your spine, legs, and feet. Notice the sensation of touching the earth, floor, or chair.

6. Remind yourself NOT to take life so personally (much easier said than done)! Life is not out to get you. Notice how frequently you take what happens as a personal affront, or as proof that something is wrong with you. Those reactions are based on the past—on old stories. Are they what you want to believe now? Be gentle with yourself as you explore these questions. Sure, the reactive

patterns are familiar, but they probably don't represent the kind of life you want, or the person that you truly are. This process allows you to explore your options.

7. Ask yourself: What are some possible alternatives to the experience I'm having? Calmness? Steadiness? Clarity? Warmth? Connectedness? Ask your upset part if it will relax and make some room for a more centered part of yourself. If you weren't collapsing or attacking right now, how else might you respond to the situation? How have others whom you admire managed in similar situations?

8. Even if you don't know what it is to be compassionate with yourself, ponder the question: What might compassion be/feel like?

9. Call on your observing self. Notice when and how these issues come up in other areas of your life. When have you successfully handled this kind of situation in the past? What helped you then? How might mastering this situation now facilitate ease in future situations?

10. Even if your physiology is out of whack, slowly practice taking charge. Imagine what it would be like to know you were in control of your life experience. Neither your fears nor your physiology needs to control your life or your relationships. Master the ability to shift perspective. Remind yourself that this will change; the feelings will ease; my physiology will return to a state of equilibrium. Behave in ways that you will later respect.

11. Separate the facts from the feelings. State the facts. Restate the facts. What feelings do you have toward those facts?

12. Separate the past from the present. Look around you, what do you see? How old are you in this moment? If the situation feels overly charged, it probably involves being triggered by associations to the past. The pull is strong, I know, but you don't have to go there! There are simple statements you can say to yourself that can preempt the tendency to regress. If you couple the statements with a determination not to re-traumatize yourself, you can, with practice, avoid many needless painful moments.

Five Key Statements:
- The danger is NOT happening now.
- Something old is being triggered.
- This is about the past.
- If it's this bad now; it gives me a sense of how hard it was then.
- I will not allow my history to keep me from living the life I want now.

13. Put the brakes on activation. Try refusing to escalate or act out. As wonderful and viscerally satisfying it may feel to get absorbed in the activation, remind yourself of all the ways acting out backfires. It almost always keeps you spinning in pain longer than necessary.

    Counteract activation by concentrating on finding pleasure in calm, strength, and self-determination, rather than getting pleasure from being perverse, going one up or one down, or being tough and uncaring. Control escalation through refusing to catastrophize, to becoming outraged, or indulging in self-righteousness. Self-criticism, blaming yourself or others (such as "I can't believe this!" "This is unacceptable!" "You're a complete idiot!") may feel satisfying in the moment, but such condemnation rarely brings you a better quality of life.

14. Develop nurturing friendships, hobbies, and physical activities. Learn to play and have fun. Actively search out events, situations, and people that draw out the best in you.

15. Refrain from turning to food, relying on substances, over-exercising, or indulging in endless catharsis of "feeling your feelings." These forms are not self-soothing; they will keep you on the hamster wheel of overreaction, rather than lead you toward a calmer and happier state.

16. Learn all the sneaky ways you defend yourself, bully others, collapse, become a victim, and deflect what's true—all so you don't have to face yourself. When you stand in the truth of your life, even as you are trying to understand how difficult it often is, then you become less fearful of being truly alive. Building self-compassion is THE essential ingredient of healing.

17. I answer your questions during my Facebook Live talks. If you'd like to follow me on Facebook you'll find me at: dfay.com/Facebook

EXERCISE: SELF-SOOTHING

Goals of Exercise:
1. Dis-identify from the troubling parts/states of mind
2. Validate these parts' experiences

It's critical that we practice being compassionate as we are making contact with different parts of us. When we feel that we need to change ourselves to be accepted, an almost automatic resistance is initiated. As our internal parts feel welcomed, and don't feel as if they need to change to be accepted, they begin to introduce themselves to teach us how they came to be. When we meet ourselves exactly where we are, without trying to change anything, these parts slowly begin to learn they aren't stuck in the role that they've adopted.

All "parts" models recognize the activated part is not the whole. If you're finding yourself stuck in an activated or shut down part, invite in the opposite quality. If angry, what would be [what I call] a more nourishing opposite? Might the opposite be calmness? Or compassion? If you're shut down, what would be more nourishing? Perhaps to become curious? Willing to take risks? Having the courage to peer into the dark void? Or maybe when you're shut down, a more nourishing opposite would be connection—being attuned to.

That attunement is exactly what you're doing when you dis-identify from the activated part and ask it what it needs, looking to provide a more nourishing component. The goal is to integrate what's been split off and resolve the pain that's been buried. Occasionally, this befriending process is easier with some parts than others. Generally, the greater the undigested charge, the more centered and grounded we need to be to avoid getting lost or overwhelmed when interacting with that part.

Center Yourself: Find a quiet place where you can reflect in relative peace. Take several slow breaths. Remind yourself that you are doing healing work and that it's important to find a way to embody some compassion or kindness. This understanding quality is a part of you that is connected and knows the way through this difficulty. If you have trouble finding that aspect within yourself, think about someone who seems to gracefully embody their own wisdom (perhaps a family member, a good friend, your therapist, or a spiritual figure). Whoever that is for you, think of that person or that quality. Notice what happens in your body as you bring this person or quality to mind. Does your breathing quiet? Do you feel less alone? If you are feeling agitated, ask that agitation, numbness, or overwhelm to step back (using IFS language)—to give yourself breathing room so you can be present. Exiled parts often slow down when they feel heard and understood. By indicating that we want to be present with them, while also acknowledging that we're feeling overloaded, a mutuality is created.

Contact Your Inner Self: As you feel yourself becoming more grounded and centered, notice your internal experience. Let whatever arises come to your attention. Is it dead quiet, or a screaming cacophony? Or do you notice the tension of a shoulder muscle? Do you feel numb? Perhaps you notice some internal screaming. Or maybe the contact provides some calm. Whatever it is, bring your attention to it.

Dis-identify from the Part: One of the hardest things to learn in trauma healing is: We are not the part/state/experience/feeling/symptom that has taken over us. These past states are hugely compelling. Remember that if, as a five-year-old, you were in a terrifying situation, you probably segregated that terror and cordoned it off in your mind. Not consciously, of course, but it was a phenomenal way to survive. As we live our lives, these parts occasionally take over, and we literally feel as if we are the terror, the numbness, the anger. Our task in these moments is to dis-identify from those past states or Parallel Lives. An easy and empowering way to do this is to name it as a part ("part holding the terror') and externalize it, such as drawing it. As you look at what you've drawn, it's easier to believe that internal experience is separate from you.

When we start practicing being ourselves, instead of identifying as just one part or another, it's important that we not befriend our most formidable parts first. Those parts don't usually give us much choice; they tug at us powerfully, not wanting to feel alone, abandoned, or betrayed. If we can, it's helpful to realize that these parts come on strongly because they sometimes desperately want us to "know" something. They want to communicate something to us and only know how to do that by flooding us with their experience. That flooding sensation represents the lack of context and understanding our younger selves were able to provide for that event. These powerful memories are taken as-is and disposed of by our ego—to help us restore order until the day comes when we're able to meet it with some compassion.

If you're having trouble dis-identifying from a part, it is helpful to send *metta,* "May you be at peace," "May you feel safe," to the intruding part. Say the phrases deliberately and intentionally to let that part know you're present. In this way, you also create distance to avoid being consumed or overwhelmed by that part.

Externalize a Part: As you feel settled, invite one part or another to become present in your awareness. Something might pop up right away, or it may take a moment for you to become aware of a part that you would like to befriend. Perhaps this is a part you feel is ready and willing to be approached with curiosity.

For example, one of my clients was describing a part that shuts down in relationships. She feels numb when this happens. I had her imagine the numb part that wanted to be understood and had her draw or write about it. By externalizing it, we "see" or "hear" an image or expression associated with the part. The part might be a certain age, or it may be linked to a specific environment or place. This part might have something to say, or it may be feeling some emotion strongly. Is there a part in you that wants to be understood? Imagine what it looks like. Write or draw something that resonates with the sensations you're feeling and where those sensations are making themselves known within your body.

Listen: What is it that this part is communicating to you? Pain? Terror? Anger? Distress? Joy? Happiness? Does it communicate through words, feelings, sensations, or images?

Sometimes parts flood us with their feelings so that we experience their entrapped emotional state. When we can stay in our frontal lobe—in our wise self—we are more able to be present to that aspect without being overwhelmed. In these moments, remind yourself to breathe. Remember, you are not the part; the part is simply communicating its experience to you, so you can help hold it, heal it, and integrate it within yourself.

Notice your response to this communication. Notice your reactions. Then take a breath, exhale slowly, and make some space inside. If need be, remind yourself that you are centered in your adult self.

Validate: What is it that this part needs to hear or feel from you? Is it reassurance that you are willing to listen? Does it want to be "held?" Is it seeking to hear words of comfort? Is it a special song that this part wants you to sing to it? Be as authentic as you can be and notice your response.

Sometimes we are afraid of a part. Can you be honest with this part—without judging it or making it wrong? Let it know that you see it, hear it, and understand it, but that you're also feeling scared of the emotions engendered by the part when it comes calling. Remind yourself, and this part, that you are willing to care for it. Acknowledge if that is so, that you are traveling a new path and you're learning new techniques to help yourself heal.

Attend to the Part Again: Notice, again, how this part responds to your communication. Does it flinch? Relax? Cry harder? Remain in your adult self as best you can, using every resource to soothe, care for, and respond compassionately to this part.

Overarching Holding: Be mindful that, even as your adult self, this process takes time. Re-learning trust may take many small moments of being tested and building your capacity to stay centered. Always return to the centered, loving, adult place of wisdom. ***Remember that patience is a virtue and a balm!***

SKILL 7: CARVING OUT A NEW PATH

Objectives:
- Continue integrating and practicing previous skills
- Generate new directions based on greater awareness
- Attach value to the new directions
- Anticipate resistance, so attempts at moving forward aren't derailed
- Identify baby steps that lead to larger successes
- Find ways of supporting those steps
- Discover "choice points" that offer alternative ways of being

Human beings can improve our understanding of internal thoughts, feelings, and body sensations, thereby changing the course of our lives. This is good news for trauma survivors, as we often feel painfully trapped by our histories.

In addition to the skills we've already discussed—concentration or being able to focus, mindfulness, the ability to dis-identify from experience through observation, separating out facts from feelings, and distinguishing past from present to remain in the present moment—we must harness our energy constructively and positively. To do this, it's good to take charge of the energy state associated with limbic dysregulation, open to our executive functioning, and awaken our heart to hold and direct the powerful energy inside our bodies.

If you are interested in working one-on-one with a Becoming Safely Embodied Skills (BSE) Certified Practitioner, specially trained to help heal challenging patterns and create inner structure to live a more fulfilling life, review our list of international providers by typing the following link into a web browser: dfay.com/cp

Old Familiar Path

We all have old familiar ways of processing our thoughts, feelings, and sensations. This is especially true when we're triggered. That's when we tend to default to patterns of negative self-talk that become oddly comfortable. Without new information, triggered parts are reluctant to change the old behaviors. Inertia has set in and the fear of the testing out something new—stepping out of our comfort zone—exceeds the discomfort of being stuck with what they don't like. The new is perceived as riskier.

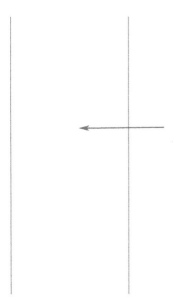

END UP IN OLD,
FAMILIAR PLACE
(usually doesn't feel
that good)

• People describe this as comfortable even if it doesn't feel that good, like wearing an old grungy pair of sweats.

• The behaviors we do on this old, familiar path may help us feel better in the short term.

• As we do the same thing, over and over again, though, we feel less soothed and more stuck.

What's Calling Us?

We're always feeling the impetus to try something, to stretch and grow. That's a fundamental experience of being a human being. We see something and feel the inner pull toward it. We sense something and seek out ways to be with that. Learning to listen to this inner call orients us in a new direction. But then, there's the need to take the next step. That's when we hesitate. That's when we feel the uncertainty of stepping into the unknown. Unless we practice in small steady ways, and create a map for entering the unknown—and how we tend to turn away from that new experience—it's easy to waffle, to stay in the old, even though it's constraining and no longer what we want.

What then could be out there in the new frontier? What could be better than what you already have? Why would you want to step into the unknown? What's compelling you, from inside, to explore something new?

It's easy at this point to find something big, something bold, something incredibly grand to be drawn to. For many people, this is a way to keep something safely impossible from ever having. So, instead, how can you make what you want small enough that you can take baby steps to get there? What might be one small step to explore, that is just the right size that your energy lifts, and you become curious about finding out more?

OLD, FAMILIAR PLACE

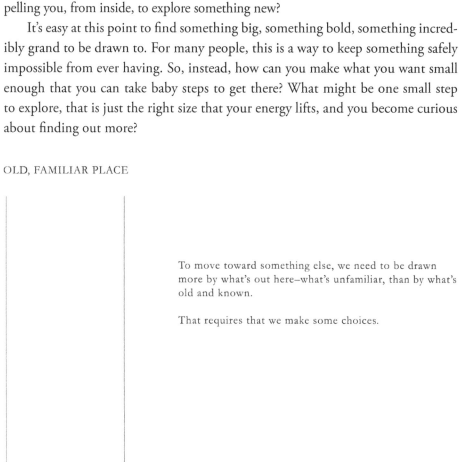

To move toward something else, we need to be drawn more by what's out here—what's unfamiliar, than by what's old and known.

That requires that we make some choices.

Choice Points

Every moment in our life offers an opportunity to find a new choice point: the exploration of a new thought, feeling, sensation, movement, impulse, behavior—anything that might reveal a new path. Gardeners know the experience of seeing an overgrown patch of ground turned slowly into a beautiful garden. Each handful of weeds picked opens new territory and creates a blank slate. It's the same with our inner world.

OLD, FAMILIAR PLACE

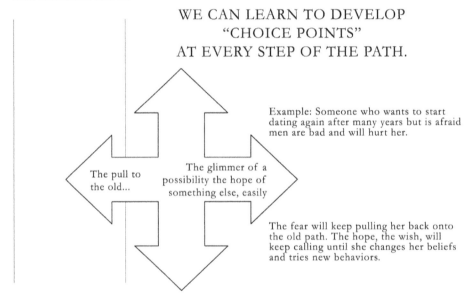

WE CAN LEARN TO DEVELOP
"CHOICE POINTS"
AT EVERY STEP OF THE PATH.

Example: Someone who wants to start dating again after many years but is afraid men are bad and will hurt her.

The pull to the old...

The glimmer of a possibility the hope of something else, easily

The fear will keep pulling her back onto the old path. The hope, the wish, will keep calling until she changes her beliefs and tries new behaviors.

Turbulence

As we identify new avenues to pursue, which could be as simple as "I want to feel better than I do now," you'll inevitably notice turbulence. Anytime we step toward something new, and attempt to let go of the old, we experience turbulence. Some people experience heightened anxiety, depression, fear, fatigue, or even terror. The intensity of those feelings will turn us back from taking the next steps into the unknown. The strength of the protective parts, the power of our internal defenses to stay safe, will urge us to turn back. It takes a lot of clarity, will, and courage at this point to anticipate the turbulence that tends to show up in our lives. When we recognize what keeps us unsatisfied, yet in our comfort zone, we can use mindfulness to name it, then harness the power of concentration to focus on where we want to go.

OLD, FAMILIAR PLACE

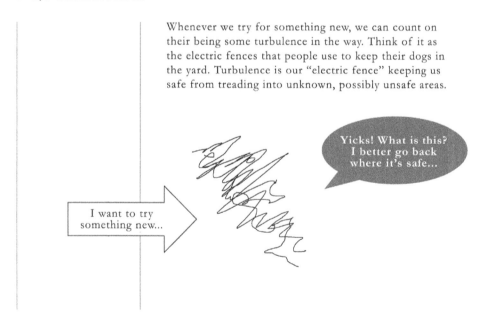

Whenever we try for something new, we can count on their being some turbulence in the way. Think of it as the electric fences that people use to keep their dogs in the yard. Turbulence is our "electric fence" keeping us safe from treading into unknown, possibly unsafe areas.

Yicks! What is this? I better go back where it's safe...

I want to try something new...

Baby Steps

Taking big steps increases the likelihood we'll be hijacked by turbulence, instead of befriending it. Taking tiny steps that build on each other slowly, gently moves us in the desired direction, while at the same time minimizing upset and resistance. We harness the power of mindfulness (naming), concentrating on just taking this one step, aware of the thoughts, feelings, and sensations that are there. Breathe. And prepare for the next small step.

OLD, FAMILIAR PLACE

To get through the turbulence, you need to try using small, baby steps instead of trying to make huge leaps over tall buildings.

Baby steps help you build a strong foundation, help build trust and confidence that you can encounter whatever arises.

It's important to know that you can go into the turbulence–and you can get back out–even if it means going back to what's safe–the old familiar path.

It's like Hansel and Gretel putting down bread crumbs as they go into the dark forest–trusting those crumbs will guide them out again.

PUTTING IT ALL TOGETHER REFLECTION

Take a moment to jot down a few thoughts in response to the following questions.

Intimately describe your old path. What thoughts, feelings, and sensations (T/F/S) have been present on this path?

_____

_____

_____

_____

_____

What alternative path would you prefer?

_____

_____

_____

_____

_____

What would be a baby step be in that direction?

_____

_____

_____

_____

_____

As you take that first step, what T/F/S do you notice?

_____

_____

_____

_____

_____

What experience (T/F/S) arises to seduce you back to the old, familiar path?

_____

_____

_____

_____

_____

How can you support yourself once you've begun this process? What T/F/S feel good, or aren't disruptive to the rest of your system? How can you reinforce your initial effort? Describe how you would support yourself as you explore this new path.

_____

_____

_____

_____

_____

What other baby steps would be necessary to keep yourself moving in the desired direction? What would that be like? If you don't feel ready, how could you make the step even smaller? How could you make it so small that the next step is the simple "of course I can" step?

_____

_____

_____

_____

_____

Learn from what you are exploring. How could you take this incremental step again? Practice it once or twice a day.

_____

_____

_____

_____

_____

CARVING OUT A NEW PATH REFLECTION

Take a moment to jot down a few thoughts in response to the following questions.

So, you're caught in a pattern. You're not feeling good. In fact, you're feeling rotten. You've heard that we all have the chance (or choice) to feel good in every moment. This process is abetted when we take advantage of "choice points" that allow us to carve out a new path. You think it's nuts, but you're willing to try it. Check it out and see how it works.

The goal is to find a way of feeling better—exactly where you are. Let's take stock of the situation. Where are you now? You're feeling crummy, but it's familiar, right? Comfortable in a strange way? This is not about jumping ahead of yourself, or even about looking good for yourself (or for the sake of others). It's about staying in the moment and looking for the choice point. Choice points are where your power lies.

Here are some steps to change your experience.

Initially, this process may feel as if you are carving out a new footpath in the rainforest. The first move is literally like using a machete to hack out a path through the underbrush. It doesn't seem like there's a way through—hence the metaphor of carving! You need to carve out the new path.

Get clear about your inner state. What thoughts, feelings, and body sensations are you having? Reach for the closest, most easily accessible thought that will reassure you and make you feel better about yourself or your situation. What is it? For example, "I'm doing the best I can," or "Things always change," or "Often the improvements are too small to notice, but I'm willing to try."

_____

_____

_____

_____

_____

How do you feel when you think of an accessible, good feeling or thought? Where does that thought reside in your body? Describe it as fully as possible using as many adjectives as you can.

_____

_____

_____

_____

_____

What's it like to feel a little bit better than you were feeling only moments ago? Remember it's not about taking giant steps. Depending on your perception, taking baby steps may even feel overwhelming. Remember that each little step matters, even though the whole process plays out gradually!

The Pull of the Pattern . . .

You'll notice that holding on to positive feelings and thoughts in the beginning is difficult. Imagine standing in front of that thick, dense forest. Your back is aching from hacking at all those branches. Standing there, rubbing your back or your arm, you visualize that familiar, well-trodden road you were thinking of leaving behind. And up crops, "What was I thinking? Why carve out a new path? It's too much work. It's easier to just stay on the old road. It's not a pleasant path, but it's already built, and what's more, I'm used to it."

That gravitational pull to stay with an old habit or pattern represents *a choice point.* See the little path you've started. Reach for a thought that makes you feel good about what you've just accomplished. Staying with the forest analogy, you might say to yourself, "The green foliage sure looks pretty." Emphasizing the positive helps release tension. Another thought might be, "Isn't it amazing how resilient these plants are?" And with that thought (and others like it), you may feel a sense of wonderment and an opening to new possibility.

Although you're not really facing an actual rainforest, you are exploring new terrain—and that is significant. Recall the thought that was making you feel better just a moment ago.

Reconnect with your body and feelings. What's happening now? Has some uneasiness resurfaced? If so, remind yourself of your choices, right here in this red-hot second. Reach for the next thought that makes you feel good about this moment.

Rhonda: I am noticing my breath a lot these days. That's the small, simple step I am learning to take without overwhelming myself. Sometimes I do this when my mind is running away with itself, or with me! And I turn my attention to my breathing. I do this at time to try and counteract unhelpful, fearful, or fear-driven thinking, and sometimes it's an attempt to lessen anxiety and/or tension. I'm finding it's like an easy, available friend I have. Though there are times when focusing on my breath causes my heart to beat faster. Then I stop focusing on my breath, or I try to let my heart rate readjust. I don't know why that happens, or when it will re-regulate itself. Still, mostly, I find breath work helpful and even necessary these days.

Matt: When I first started doing this work, I was always triggered in some way, causing my heart to beat faster. I found that something that was supposed to make me feel at ease, did the opposite—it made me aware of my body, which can be very triggering, and made it harder for me to breathe. Since then, I've learned to slow down. A LOT! I take more time. I actively seek out the pleasure of being present. I still can't really focus as much as I'd like, so I've been learning to enjoy the small moments that I am present, which gives me the courage to extend that time. It kind of resets me. I'm not caught in the misery of constantly swirling in my activated parts. It reminds me of when I turn off my cell phone and restart it when it's acting quirky. Once it comes back online, things seem to be working better.

Jeff: I'm learning to receive good things. Now I take a moment, or longer, to really let something good sink in; it's an awareness I have now—to not skip over it. And I relate a lot to using breath to be more present. Sometimes I find that focusing on my breath allows me to take time out of things that I am not in control of, giving me a moment to pause, at least in the moment.

Describe a typical pattern that often plays out in your life.

Example: A woman who is dating tends to get anxious or fearful.

Pattern	Next Steps	Impact on her	Outcome
Wants partner / companion / family	Realizes she needs to meet a potential partner for this to happen	Thinking about this increases her anxiety	The more she thinks about it, the greater her anxiety. She spirals into feeling trapped and terrified.

How she might intervene in this pattern?

Pattern	Next Steps	Impact on her	Outcome
Wants partner / companion / family	Realizes she needs to meet a potential partner for this to happen. Gets anxious thinking about meeting a potential partner.	Notes the anxiety. Intervenes through breathing. Does some self-soothing. Recognizes the turbulence she's feeling. Looks for a baby step.	Decides to smile at one person a day and be excited that she could do that, rather than freaking out about all the other things she could/ should be doing. Another option would be looking at pictures of people in magazines and making up positive stories about them.

What about YOUR patterns? Where do you get stuck? What do you want to shift? Name as many of them as you can.

_____

_____

_____

_____

_____

Think of three things in your life that you want to be different. For each of them, describe what you want to be different and why you want it to be different.

_____

_____

_____

_____

_____

Notice: What is the way it is now? What do you want to be different? Why do you want to make the change?

_____

_____

_____

_____

_____

FEELING GOOD VS. FEELING BAD REFLECTION

Take a moment to jot down a few thoughts in response to the following questions.

In any moment we have the power to shift toward what we want, rather than remain feeling stuck. All it takes (the statement is simple, the practice profound) is practicing feeling good, instead of feeling bad. We do that by noticing what we are feeling/thinking/sensing inside ourselves. What is it for you right now?

_____

_____

_____

―――――――――――――――――――――――――――――――
―――――――――――――――――――――――――――――――

What would you rather have? Flesh out the details with as much sensory information as possible (how it feels, looks, smells, sounds).

―――――――――――――――――――――――――――――――
―――――――――――――――――――――――――――――――
―――――――――――――――――――――――――――――――
―――――――――――――――――――――――――――――――
―――――――――――――――――――――――――――――――

Write down all the reasons WHY you want this, using as many pages as you like.
Your goal in this exercise is just to feel good.

―――――――――――――――――――――――――――――――
―――――――――――――――――――――――――――――――
―――――――――――――――――――――――――――――――
―――――――――――――――――――――――――――――――
―――――――――――――――――――――――――――――――

Notice how you feel as you write. Better? Worse? About the same? If you are
fully engaged in the experience, chances are that you're feeling better. Or if you're
having trouble, strengthen your capacity to focus on what you want, rather than
defaulting to feelings of being stuck with what you have. If "impossible thinking"
arises (and it probably will), transition from those thoughts to what you want,
and why you want it. This focuses you on what makes you feel good. When you
identify those, pause, and revel in those feelings. This approach allows you to build
some energy to shift your thinking . . . so thinking of what you want doesn't feel
impossible any longer.

What do you want to be different?	Give reasons. Embellish with details about what would be wonderful if this change took place. Phrase positively.	Notice the experience in your body. How do you know that it feels good? (Use colorful, expressive, uplifting language.)	How does this move you toward feeling good? Also, what helps you continue to focus on feeling good?	What derails your good feelings? How do you find a choice point to feel good again?
I want to have a new apartment.	*I'd love to have lots of space to put things, to see the sun flood through the windows, to have a solid front door so I'd feel safe.*	*I feel a little smile on my lips. I feel brighter, slightly happier— more cheerful.*	*Thinking that something like this is possible is amazing.* *Having the images of the sunlight, imagining plants, feeling safe—these really help.*	*Worrying that I won't find such a nice place brings me down.* *A choice point might be to remember there are all kinds of places out there; finding a nicer place is just as possible as finding the one I have now.*

(Fill in your own experience)				

STEPPING-STONES/DREAM LIST REFLECTION

Take a moment to jot down a few thoughts in response to the following questions.

Once we know where we don't want to go, we need to orient ourselves toward someplace positive. If we don't have a sense of where we *do* want to go, we will consistently be re-directed back to the old path, the old habit, and the old way of thinking.

Take time to explore how you can move toward a life that feels better, a life that is outside the pattern of your traumatic history. Let's look at how you can take baby steps toward the life you really want to live.

It starts with finding something to orient toward, something that feels better than where you are. Let's investigate states-of-being that make you feel more relaxed, perhaps even happier or more joyful. You'll need something "good" to orient toward, to hold your ground when the turbulence begins. Remember, whenever you move outside your normal, familiar range, you'll feel some turbulence. For some it will be anxiety, for others depression, while others might notice it as an adrenaline rush.

Take note of where you are, physically and emotionally. This may include the process of knowing exactly who or what is here inside—that is, paying attention to all the different parts that make up your experience in the moment. You may notice aspects that are elevated, bored, distressed, hopeful, anxious, relaxed, doubtful, whatever.

_____

_____

_____

Take about five minutes. During that time, make a list of everything you can think of that makes you feel better. Include all details that make you feel more open, relaxed, happy, or enthusiastic. (Examples may include playing with your dog, petting your cat, drinking a refreshing glass of water, seeing flowers blooming that you planted in your yard, going for a swim on a hot day, and so on. This list can also include other fulfilling experiences such as nurturing relationships and interesting hobbies.) Do this without censoring, writing it as fast as you can.

_____

_____

_____

_____

_____

After five minutes, stop writing and take note of how you feel. Notice if doing this exercise changed your energy. How do you feel now about moving toward something new?

_____

_____

_____

_____

_____

_____

_____

Study the list. Remember there are no right answers or wrong things to have on this list. This is a simple practice to remember what feels good for you.

Write down your responses to the following questions:
- How do you feel about what you've written? Pleasantly surprised? Frustrated? Resistant?

_____

_____

_____

_____

_____

- Was it difficult to come up with positive ideas? Did you freeze? Was your headspace noisy? Try to describe the elements of your experience.

_____

_____

_____

_____

_____

- Does the list reflect who you really are? Or does the list reflect who you think you should be? Explain.

_____

_____

_____

_____

_____

Choose one of the items from your list. Talk with someone about what steps you might take to move toward this goal. Here are a couple of examples to get you started:

- Having more beauty in your home might mean buying flowers once a week, planting flowers in the yard, taking a painting class, or going to the museum just for inspiration.
- Feeling more connected to others might mean taking a class at the local adult education center, going to a church event, joining a book club, lingering after a group event and talking to someone, joining an online chat group, or going to a twelve-step meeting.

SKILL 8: TELLING AND RETELLING

Objectives:

- To increase awareness of our perspectives and the life stories we tell ourselves through which we perceive the world
- To suggest a new choice-point where previously there was none
- To practice looking at the world through new filters and with new thoughts
- To encourage letting go of old, encrusted, and disempowering beliefs/stories
- To start building affectively loaded stories that create new empowering neural networks
- To foster the possibility of a shift toward a more positive sense of self

Most of us look at the world from a specific and habitual perspective, formed through our thoughts and what we've been told. In this way, we emphasize those characteristics that align with familiar patterns.

If we hold these familiar thoughts to be true, eventually these thoughts and ideas become beliefs. We have a lot of evidence for why they're "true." They literally shape and color the world in which we live, because everything that occurs is interpreted based on those beliefs. Examples of beliefs might include: "It's not a safe world," "Life is too difficult," "You can't trust people," "Democrats (or Republicans) are all fools," "Men are dangerous," and "Women are manipulative." You get the idea.

These beliefs shape our reality. They predicate the windows of experiences that we look through. It's not like we're making them up. We don't mean to have limited world views. It's just that they feel so "real." We interpret the evidence to support our point of view, which of course, reinforces our beliefs. We talk to others about the situation, and they are often more than happy to agree with us and prop up our point of view. Until we question our beliefs, we cannot free ourselves of their distortion. When we do that consciously and deliberately, we slowly break apart the concreteness of the habituated version. To make choice points and move in a new direction, we must repattern our thoughts, until new beliefs form that arise from and align with our new purpose.

Michael White and David Epston (1993) first introduced me to this strategy. These extraordinary therapists in Australia and New Zealand developed Narrative Therapy: the telling and retelling of stories to find new, more wholesome perspectives. The main tenet of Narrative Therapy states that the person is never the problem; the person simply has a problem. Further, they believe that none of us want our problems; we just don't know what else to do. The telling and retelling of what's wrong compounds the feeling of being stuck.

Being able to externalize the story allows us to put a wedge into the old version and begin to make enough space to create a new, more positive outcome. It's a beautiful way to practice walking out of old concrete-encased versions of the story.

Given fresh perspectives from unusual sources, people are willing to play a little more with their internal set points, which encourages new and more empowering stories.

Any story we tell and retell gathers evidence. When we choose stories that lean in a positive direction, we can explore new choice points that invite us to explore other choices. When we repeat the same stories, we reinforce the "truth" of those stories, and consign ourselves to the old familiar path. Telling the same stories perpetuates the same outcome that makes the stories seem reliable and true. Reciting the new story to yourself, or by writing, allows the new path to emerge and seem possible.

Usually, we tell stories as a way of cataloguing and reinforcing our current, symptom-laden point of view. It's a way of gathering evidence to support a particular (known) outcome, and it reinforces our current belief structure.

Most of us don't often see our beliefs/perspectives for what they are. We've been with them for so long, we've traveled that same mental, emotional, and physical path for so long they become set "in stone." Developed in the past, they continue to exist in our now—and orient our future. These beliefs are now so deeply embedded in our body and mind that they've become the normal way of life. They're beliefs that have become reality. Seeing through such perspectives, and making changes, is difficult when we're retelling stories that reinforce old ways of seeing and knowing.

Many of us have entrenched beliefs that appear to have protected us for years. It makes it harder to release those beliefs and those fears. We don't know what would happen otherwise.

I love using the Telling and Retelling approach to invite fresh perspectives and generate new thoughts that will lead to a more empowering belief system from which to live life.

1. Tell the story of a personal event, preferably one containing an emotional charge. This is the time to embellish the story with as many feelings as possible! Write down this version of the story as much as you can. Then reflect on the story as you've written it:

- What does this story say about you now?
- Do you detect background thoughts as you tell this story?
- What are you feeling as you tell the story?
- Do you know what sensations are happening in your body?

2. The next step is to tell the story from a different perspective, maybe even with a different outcome. You might want to encourage a story with other possibilities. Alexis recounted sitting in the park with a friend, upset about something. Some children were playing by the pond. I suggested she tell the story from the children's point of view. She first started by sliding the story round to tell it from her point of view! But when I reminded her to use the children's point of view, she found herself happy, enthusiastic and joyful; she was surprised. Other options might be:

- If the dust particles in the air could tell a story, what would they say?
- How might Oprah tell it, or Bono from U2?
- What about the chair you're sitting on? How would that chair describe what happened?
- How would a pet recount the incident?
- The variations are endless—and completely fun to try.

3. As you retell the story, be attentive to the positive pieces or themes in the new story. Alexis, as she was in the park, also described seeing a hawk while she was sitting with her friend. One option could be to take on the perspective of the hawk and tell the story from its point of view. When she did so, her comments were magical. She described seeing the world free from gravity, feeling the strength of her wings as she dipped and soared in the sky. She felt expansive.

- What happens in your body when you tell the story from a different perspective?
- What thoughts are you having now? Feelings? And sensations? How do they differ from the earlier ones?

4. Repeat a third time. Find yet another perspective to explore the story from, perhaps as your fairy godmother or as a furtive mouse.

5. After three rounds, take a step back. Which version do you prefer? What combination of elements felt the best? What thoughts made you feel better? Which perspectives allowed your body to feel more relaxed, your eyes to smile, energy to expand, and orientation toward life to become more open?

6. Wonder with yourself-- what it would be like to live life from a different perspective? What if every day you tried out a new perspective? What would the effects be?

7. Actively experimenting with a new interpretation/story can be challenging when old emotional patterns are being triggered. That's exactly when a new perspective can be most helpful.

8. Remind yourself: believing what you've always believed means reacting in the same ways you've always reacted. And reacting in the same old ways means getting the same old results. The old beliefs are holding the past in place.

Telling new stories can provide you with newfound vigor to proceed in a more satisfying direction.

SUPPORTING THE PRACTICE REFLECTION

Take a moment to jot down a few thoughts in response to the following questions.

As you try out different narratives, find ways to celebrate yourself, delighting in these new ways you're being in your body.

When did you try something new instead of going down the old path? What was that like in your body? Did you have different thoughts? Feelings?

_____

_____

_____

_____

_____

How did you prepare yourself to take this step?

_____

_____

_____

_____

_____

What preparations led to it?

_____

_____

_____

_____

_____

Prior to this step, did you nearly turn back? If so, how did you stop yourself? From this vantage point, what did you notice yourself doing that might have contributed to this outcome?

_____

_____

_____

_____

_____

Share some background regarding this accomplishment. What were the circumstances surrounding this achievement? Did anyone else contribute? If so, please describe.

_____

_____

_____

_____

_____

What developments have occurred in other areas of your life that may relate to this? How do you think these developments prepared the way for you to take these steps?

_____

_____

_____

Consider how you might want to use this skill in the future. Focus on the gains and how this practice expands future possibilities.

_____
_____
_____
_____
_____

TELLING AND RETELLING REFLECTION

Based on the material of Michael White (1993)

When we are _Telling and Retelling_ (Michael White, 1993) the stories of our lives, we have an opportunity to rethink outcomes relative to previously experienced events. _Answer the following questions and notice what happens as you begin to think and tell a different story._

Think about an experience in your life that turned out differently from what you expected. What were the concrete, specific things, events that shaped the outcome?

_____
_____
_____
_____
_____

Did you do anything consciously to have the different outcome? Were there particular relationships or connections that helped you?

_____
_____
_____
_____

What occurred that almost stopped you on your path? Did you turn off course? How did you get back on course?

_____
_____
_____
_____
_____

Why is this new outcome important to you? What feels differently to you? How are your thoughts different now? Do you notice your body responding in a new way?

_____
_____
_____
_____
_____

Have you noticed yourself behaving differently in other situations? If so, describe those changes.

_____
_____
_____
_____
_____

SKILL 9: FINDING GUIDANCE FROM YOUR OLDER, WISER SELF

Objectives:

- To realize there is a way through the complicated moments in life, no matter how long they last
- To realize some part of you already knows the way and can guide and direct you to the life you want to live
- To understand this is a way to cement the previous skills you've learned, including *Carving Out a New Path: Choice Points* and taking baby steps to get there
- To anchor yourself more deeply in your own internal "knowing" of the path you're taking and the steps that will get you there
- To understand that by writing down or drawing pictures of what information you "receive," you'll have that wisdom to help guide you along the way

When we have access to our own inner wisdom, we are guided from within, taking us through the many hills and valleys of life with a stronger, more solid, secure self. Everyone has access to this wisdom inside them, but we might use have different language to describe it. Whatever language is right for you, use it. There is no right way, and there is no wrong language—no wrong description—for this connection you have to yourself.

Remind yourself that you can access your own internal wisdom to support yourself.

Certain parts may want to direct you to a negative outcome—perhaps to a horrible imagined future where you end up alone with Alzheimer's, with no one caring for you, or where you end up angry, bitter, and homeless. I address this potentiality upfront, as some parts might want to pull you in that direction.

If that does happen, ask those parts holding out for a painful future to hang out in a separate room. It's important to hear what those parts have to say, but the goal of this exercise is to support, nourish, and guide ourselves in listening to our deeper inner wisdom.

Just as elite athletes do by preparing with visualization, this meditation is a way to pre-pave, to prepare you in developing wisdom, hope, and understanding about the unique path you are living into.

EXERCISE: FINDING THE OLDER, WISER SELF

I'm going to walk you through a meditation, an exercise . . . where you imagine and then have a conversation with you, as your older, wiser self. Let me explain, but first, some guideposts:

Have art and writing materials available before you guide yourself in this meditation. Please use my narrative only as a starting point . . . feel free to explore other ways this story might unfold. Adapt it to the voice of your inner knowing.

There are two paths we can take—one is the old familiar, habitual path that leads to feeling bad, stuck, and repeating old beliefs. The other path is new, but is full of uncertainty, and may seem impossible. We may feel as if we're deluding ourselves by entertaining a trip down this path. Some parts may want to mire us in the angry, bitter, older and more acquainted part of ourselves. This, though, is a way to focus attention on a specific life-giving viewpoint. Gently, ask those parts to go to a safe space while you explore this path.

Of course, if you're not ready for this, there are other ways!

You could draw the parts that are resistant to doing this exercise. Let the colors and shapes describe your thoughts, feelings, and body sensations. Draw them in full color, with balloon callouts to hold their thoughts.

Does that give you some room to explore *finding the older, wiser self*?

If you're ready to move on, here is a suggested narrative:

We're going to be accessing your older, wiser self to see how she/he/it might guide you from the future . . . let's say when you're eighty-seven years of age. That might seem old to some of you! Younger folks can select an age that seems less out of reach. Whatever the age, we're going to contact you—as an older, wiser person who has already traveled your path. It's the part of you that has been through life, has suffered, felt the pain and terror, and yet, somehow, someway, found success, even though the path wasn't known. You often had to improvise along the way, but persisted. It's not that it was easy—there were times when she was ready to give up. It felt too hard.

Somehow, though, she made it through. She knows this path. She walked it, lived it, experienced it every step of the way. She knows something about integrating all the life experiences—all the icky times, hard times, and good times. Imagine this woman. She exists.

Allow impressions to float into your awareness, whether through thoughts, feelings, images, or body sensations. It will come to you as you open yourself to receive.

Here's the script if you want it:

Imagine this woman, you . . . Bring her to life . . .

What does she look like at the age you've chosen?

Where is she? Sitting? Standing? Is she moving?

What is her environment like? Does she live in the city? The country?

What clothes is she wearing?

What kinds of activities is she involved in?

What kind of relationships does she have? Who is important to her?

Does she read books? Magazines? What movies does she like?

As we invite all our senses into this, what does she enjoy the scent of?

Imagine her moving through her world, enjoying her senses . . .

What does she like to look at? Or touch?

Let's go visit her . . . Enter into the scene with her . . . Notice her face light up when you appear to her . . . She's always happy to see you, content when you go, delighted when you return. She always has time for you . . . She enjoys taking the time to sit with you, take walks with you.

Take the time to deepen into her presence . . . Look at the love that glows and radiates as she welcomes you into her world.

Notice what it's like for you to be with her . . . How does your body respond?

If there are parts that are scared, take a moment to reassure them, or invite them to go to a safe and loving space while you continue being in her presence.

Take time to relax into her presence . . . Experience how you relate to her. Look around, what do you see? Hear? Feel? What helps you feel comfortable with her?

As you soften and relax in her presence, take the time you need to become familiar with her.

What questions, concerns, thoughts arise within you?

What haven't you been able to ask anyone else?

What terrors linger inside you, too overwhelming to talk to anyone else about?

See her looking at you with all the love in the world, comfortable with herself and with you.

Sit down and talk to her. How close to her are you?

Let yourself be seated where you feel comfortable . . . If you want to be touched, allow her to touch you exactly as it feels safe.

Feel the steadiness of her presence . . . This is a woman who has come a long way. She's made the journey. She already knows how you are going to work it out. She knows, because she's already done it.

Feel your body relax as you understand the significance of her presence . . . She is your ally. Experience the tension leaving your body . . . However it's comfortable for you, bring her your worries, fears . . . Bring her your problems and all the turbulent, unsettled life experiences. Ask her for guidance. Let the words flow easily, or just blurt it out helter-skelter. She's fine with however you communicate. She doesn't need for you to do it right. Let her listen to you and hold your concerns . . . Notice how she responds to you . . .

What does she say? Let her comforting words fill your heart, mind, body and soul . . . When you're ready, take some time to say thank you . . . and start to bring this conversation to a close.

As you breathe in and out, by her side, feel your gratitude . . .

What happened during your visit with your older, wiser self that you appreciate?

What arose in that conversation that has nurtured you and refreshed you?

How has this experience informed your next step of the journey? Let her know. See how she receives this information.

Take a few moments to share any final thoughts with your older, wiser self.

Now, take a few breaths and rejoin our circle in the here and now.

Take some paper and write or draw what happened. Re-experience the words and the feelings as you dictate what happened in your time together.

Before we end, take a moment and see what it's like now in your body . . . What thoughts are you having? Feelings? What's the physical experience of being in your body? Do you feel confident, content, peaceful? Or are you having other thoughts, feelings and body sensations? Or perhaps you're aware that during this exercise you experienced several different things? How does your body tell you that you feel that way? Some people find it helpful to draw or write what happened as a way of solidifying the experience.

PART III
Conclusion

PRACTICE, PRACTICE, PRACTICE

Someone once asked me: "What's the best practice to deal with trauma?"

My answer was simple. Can you guess?

It's whatever practice you practice.

There are many healing modalities and many of them work. Some of them work for some, some for others. And if you're anything like me, you'll want everything to change instantly, including yourself!

I've found from working with countless people that it's only by practicing one thing frequently that you master the skills so they're available when life gets challenging.

When the heat is turned up, you need to have these skills so well developed, so ingrained, that they function almost automatically.

That means practice, practice, practice.

It's essential to practice what you hope to learn. When you practice any of these skills, they'll become more familiar and easier to remember. Eventually, they become part of procedural (habitual) memory and begin to replace old dysfunctional habits.

Actively practice every day.

It shifts the "wisdom" from someone outside you to finding your own inner wisdom. And that's the most important part of all!

Practice often.

I encourage you to practice the same skill every day for a while, so it becomes as old and familiar as the patterns you are trying to shift. Many also find it helpful to keep a journal of their experiences and re-read them at those times when using the skills is difficult.

If you are interested in working one-on-one with a Becoming Safely Embodied Skills (BSE) Certified Practitioner, specially trained to help heal challenging patterns and create inner structure to live a more fulfilling life, review our list of international providers by typing the following link into a web browser: www.dfay.com/cp

Frequently Asked Questions related to Becoming Safely Embodied

Over the past thirty years, people have written me with questions and comments. I've responded to some of them here. They might be similar to questions you have. If you don't find the answer here, I tackle your questions during my Facebook Live talks; you can find and follow me on Facebook at: www.dfay.com/faceboo k. Feel free to post questions on my Facebook page or email me at dfay@dfay.com, and I'll respond to your questions on one of my future Facebook Live sessions.

- "WHY DO YOU FOCUS ON SKILLS?"
- Many of us didn't have the good fortune to be raised by people who understood how to help a child organize his or her inner world. Once we learn these simple skills, so much of life becomes easier.
- "IT'S NOT EASY TO BE IN MY BODY. PLUS, MY MIND CAN BE SCATTERED, AND I GET HORRIBLY OVERWHELMED AT TIMES. I CAN'T IMAGINE IT CHANGING."
- Those are some of the difficult symptoms of trauma and attachment wounding. There is a simple process to healing. And these are skills to get you there. It does take practice though until those new skills become habitual. Then, when we're triggered, our body, mind, and heart have a new place to turn.
- "HOW DID YOU DEVELOP YOUR APPROACH?"
- It's an outgrowth of my own healing. Years ago, when Bessel van der Kolk asked me to create a group program at his clinic, I thought deeply about what had helped me heal many years prior. All the workshops, courses, and trainings I teach are the outgrowth of those personal inquiries, which have helped so many more in their own healing. I started teaching the Becoming Safely Embodied skills in a ten-week group, which became so helpful to people that they wanted more. I extended the groups to twenty-four weeks, and then added a second year, then a third for those who wanted to keep growing and developing. Dr. Janina Fisher kept sending her clients to the groups, saying she saw them "getting better faster." Along the way, Janina joined me in co-leading the groups.

The Question Behind the Question

Underneath the questions people ask is a deeper question: Is it possible for ME? Can I change? Is it possible for me to shift these painful patterns into a more fulfilling life? Can I truly organize this crazy inner world?

The simple answer is yes.

And it takes some work. It requires patience, practice, and believing in the possibility. It means listening to your heart—like when you were reading this and something inside quickened.

It means giving hope room to grow inside. It means nurturing the hope, giving it room to flourish. It means turning toward hope, toward the possibility that what you know deep inside should be different.

I've seen people make incredible changes in their lives. I've had therapists from all over the world tell me how their clients have changed.

It happens step by step. In many cases, it happens inch by inch! Millimeter by millimeter. And you know what? That's the best way. When we go too fast, sometimes we miss putting the tiny underlying bits into place.

The BSE system acts as both a map and guidebook. This book presents the nine core skills that can help you be more at home with your internal world, cultivate a body that's a safe place for rest, reflection, and wellbeing, and take steps to create the life you want to live, instead of living in the life your history catapults you into.

If you are an individual on your own healing path and are interested in using these skills in a deeper way, there is a wealth of opportunity to learn, grow, and flourish using the Becoming Safely Embodied skills. There have been many people who have shared their stories throughout the years of picking up this book and trying just one thing, finding that one thing made all the difference. It's something we consistently hear from those who have read this book, taken the Becoming Safely Embodied online skills course, or joined our groups.

Want to hear some inspiring stories or explore additional free resources? I'd love to share them with you, so I've created a special resources section online!

To access the FREE online book bonuses type the following link into a web browser:

www.dfay.com/resources

Once you join, I'll follow up with a series of emails going even more deeply into the subject. I even have a couple of surprises for you. So, join now!

Sending goodness,

Deirdre Fay

www.dfay.com/resources

MOMENTS OF GRATITUDE

Take a moment to jot down a few thoughts in response to the following questions.

There's research about the power of gratitude as a guiding gift in our lives. Here's a way to explore using gratitude as a practice in your life. As you've been going through these skills, exploring how they support you in Becoming Safely Embodied, what stands out for you?

Take some time to draw or write what's emerged during this time. It might be a new possibility, a new sense of something, a connection discovered that was missing earlier, a skill that you used, or some combination. Take whatever time you need and put that into words, shapes, or drawings.

What words come to you? Images? Feelings?

_____

_____

_____

_____

_____

What's that like to settle into that? How does your body respond?

_____

_____

_____

_____

_____

Now think of people in your life that you are grateful for. What small or big experiences created that gratitude? Make a note of those people. What one thing (there may be many, but choose one) are you most grateful to them for?

_____

_____

_____

_____

_____

Write a note or draw them a card with a simple expression of gratitude. It might just be one word, it might be a sentence or paragraph, or a whole letter. Put it in an envelope and send it off to them. Or make a short video expressing your gratitude to them on your phone. Don't forget to email it to them!

_____
_____
_____
_____
_____

What happens in you as you sit with gratitude?

_____
_____
_____
_____
_____

My gratitude is to you. For having the courage to be on the healing path. To be willing to undertake the enormous journey of becoming more fully you. Each of us has the path already available to us . . . inside us. That's what will guide each of us.

May love come to meet you every day of your life. May every step be lit with the light of consciousness as it guides you. Trust that your heart is reaching for you. Your heart is saying there's a way through. Listen to yourself. Your heart is your guide. You can trust that. Even as your heart takes you through many messes, the purpose is to bring you back home to yourself in a solid, powerful way. Trust that.

You are not alone. You have the gift of your own being inside. And your heart will always call to you. Always. Through a thousand years and a thousand lifetimes you are being guided, from within. Listen. Listen to yourself. Listen to your heart.

INDEX OF REFLECTIONS, JOURNALING AND EXERCISES

―――――――――

Reflections/Journaling

Exercises

ADDITIONAL RESOURCES

To join Deirdre Fay's mailing list, go to: www.dfay.com/safeguide

From Foreword

Ogden, P., Minton, K, and Pain, P. (2006) Trauma and the body: a sensorimotor approach to psychotherapy. New York: Norton.

Van der Kolk, B. A., McFarlane, A., & Elisabeth, L. (1996). "Traumatic stress: The effects of overwhelming experience on mind, body and society." New York: Guilford Press.

Van der Kolk, B. A. & Filler, R. (1995). "Dissociation and the fragmentary nature of traumatic memories: overview and exploratory study." *Journal of Traumatic Stress,* 8(4), 505-525.

From Content

Agazarian, Y. (1997). *Systems-centered therapy for groups.* New York: Guilford Press.

Ainsworth, M. D. S., Blehar, M. C., Waters, E., & Wall, S. (1978). *Patterns of attachment: A psychological study of the strange situation.* Hillsdale, NJ: Lawrence Erlbaum Associates, Inc.

Aposhyan, S. (2007). *Natural intelligence: Body-mind integration and human development.* Boulder, CO: NOW Press.

Aposhyan, S. (2004). *Body-mind psychotherapy: Principles, techniques, and practical applications.* New York: W. W. Norton & Company.

Assagioli, R. (1988/2007). *Transpersonal development: The dimension beyond psychosynthesis.* Forres, UK: Smiling Wisdom/Inner Way Productions.

Barks, C. (1995). *The essential Rumi.* New York: HarperCollins.

Beckes, L., IJzerman, H., & Tops, M. (2015). Toward a radically embodied neuroscience of attachment and relationships. *Frontiers in Human Neuroscience, 9,* 266.

Begley, S. (2007). *Train Your Mind, Change Your Brain: How a New Science Reveals Our Extraordinary Potential to Transform Ourselves.* New York, NY: Ballentine Books.

Bowlby, J. (1969). *Attachment and loss, Vol. 1: Loss.* New York: Basic Books.

Bowlby, J. (1973). *Attachment and loss, Vol. 2: Separation.* New York: Basic Books.

Bowlby, J. (1979). *The making and breaking of affectional bonds.* New York: Brunner-Routledge.

Bowlby, John (1980). *Attachment and loss, Vol. 3: Loss, sadness, and depression.* New York: Basic Books.

Bremner, J. D. & Marmar, C. R. (Eds.). (1998). *Trauma, memory, and dissociation.* Washington, D.C.: American Psychological Association.

Bretherton, I., (1992). The origins of attachment theory: John Bowlby and Mary Ainsworth. *Developmental Psychology, 28,* 759–775.

Bretherton, I. & Munholland, K. A. (1999). Internal working models revisited. In J. Cassidy & P. R. Shaver (Eds.). *Handbook of attachment: Theory, research, and clinical applications* (pp. 89– 111). New York: Guilford Press.

Bromberg, P. (2011). *The Shadow of the tsunami and the growth of the relational mind.* New York: Routledge.

Brown, D. (2012). Peak Performance Workshop. Harvard University Continuing Education Conference notes and handouts. Boston.

Brown, R. & Gerbarg, P. (2012). *The healing power of the breath: Simple techniques to reduce stress and anxiety, enhance concentration, and balance your emotions.* Boston: Shambhala Publications.

Brown, D. (2005–2015). Attachment seminar. Newton, MA.

Brown, D., Elliott, D., et al. (2016). *Attachment disturbances in adults: Treatment for comprehensive repair.* New York: W. W. Norton & Company.

Brown, D. (2013). Workshop: Meditation & visualization practices for everyday living & well-being and to enhance peak performance. Boston, MA: Harvard Medical School Department of Continuing Education

Campbell, J. & Moyers, B. (1991). *The power of myth* (p. 149). New York: Anchor Books.

Chu, J. (1998). *Rebuilding shattered lives: The responsible treatment of complex post-traumatic stress and dissociative disorders.* New York: Guilford Press.

Corrigan, F. (2014). Shame and the Vestigial Midbrain Urge to Withdraw. In Lanius, U., Paulsen, S., & Corrigan, F. *Neurobiology and treatment of traumatic dissociation: Toward an embodied self.* (pp.173-191). New York: Springer Publishing.

Corrigan, F., Wilson, A., & Fay, D. (2014a). Attachment and Attachment Repair. In Lanius, U., Paulsen, S., & Corrigan, F. *Neurobiology and treatment of traumatic dissociation: Toward an embodied self* (pp. 193–212). New York: Springer Publishing.

Corrigan, F., Wilson, A., & Fay, D. (2014b). The compassionate self. In: Lanius, U., Paulsen, S., & Corrigan, F. (Eds.). *Neurobiology and treatment of traumatic dissociation: Toward an embodied self* (pp. 269–288). New York: Springer Publishing.

Elliott, S. & Edmonson, D. (2005). *The new science of breath.* Allen, TX: Coherence Press.

Fay, D. (2017). *Attachment-Based Yoga & Meditation for Trauma Recovery.* New York: W.W.Norton & Company.

Fay, D. (2015). *Trauma, attachment, & Yoga training manual.*

Fay, D. (2007). *The Becoming Safely Embodied skills manual.* Boston: Heartfull Press.

Fay, D. (1986). The Becoming Safely Embodied skills handouts. Watertown, MA.

Fisher, J. (2017). *Healing the fragmented selves of trauma survivors: Overcoming internal self-alienation.* New York: Routledge.

Fisher, J. (2015). *Dissociative phenomena in the everyday lives of trauma survivors.* Paper presented at the Boston University Medical School.

Fisher, J. (2013). *Overcoming trauma-related shame and self-loathing.* Eau Claire, WI: CMI Education-PESI Workshop.

Fisher, J. (2010). *Psychoeducational aids for treating psychological trauma.* Cambridge, MA: Kendall Press.

Freedman, J. & Combs, G. (1996). *Narrative Therapy: The Social Construction of Preferred Realities.* New York, NY: W. W. Norton & Company.

Gendlin, E. (1978). *Focusing.* New York: Bantam Dell.

Germer, C. & Neff, K. (2014). Mindful Self-Compassion (MSC) Teacher Guide. San Diego, CA: Center for Mindful Self-Compassion.

Germer, Christopher. (2009). *The mindful path to self-compassion: Freeing yourself from destructive thoughts and emotions.* New York: Guilford Press.

Germer, C. K. & Neff, K. D. (2013). Self-compassion in clinical practice. *Journal of Clinical Psychology, 69,* 856–867. doi: 10.1002/jclp.22021.

Gilbert, P. (1997). The evolution of social attractiveness and its role in shame, humiliation, guilt and therapy. *British Journal of Medical Psychology, 70,* 113–147.

Gilbert, P. (1998). What is shame? Some core issues and controversies. In P. Gilbert, & B. Andrews (Eds.). *Shame: Interpersonal behavior, psychopathology, and culture* (pp. 3–36). New York: Oxford University Press.

Gilbert, P. (2003). Evolution, social roles, and differences in shame and guilt. *Social Research, 70,* 1205–1230.

Gilbert, P. (Ed.) (2005). *Compassion: Conceptualisations, research and use in psychotherapy.* London: Routledge.

Gilbert, P. (2007). *Psychotherapy and counselling for depression,* 3rd Ed. London: Sage.

Gilbert, P. (2009a). *The compassionate mind.* Oakland, CA: New Harbinger Publications.

Gilbert, P. (2009b). The nature and basis for compassion focused therapy. *Hellenic Journal of Psychology, 6,* 273–291.

Gilbert, P. (2009c). Introducing compassion-focused therapy. *Advances in Psychiatric Treatment 15,* 199–208.

Gilbert, P. (2010). *Compassion focused therapy: The CBT distinctive features series.* London, UK: Routledge.

Gilbert, P. & Choden. (2014). *Mindful Compassion: How the science of compassion can help you understand your emotions, live in the present, and connect deeply with others.* Oakland, CA: New Harbinger Publications.

Gilbert, P. & Irons, C. (2005). Focused therapies and compassionate mind training for shame and self-attacking. In, P. Gilbert (Ed.). *Compassion: Conceptualisations, research and use in psychotherapy* (263–325). London, UK: Routledge.

Gilbert, P., McEwan, K., Matos, N., & Rivis, A. (2011). Fears of compassion: Development of three self-report measures. *Psychology and Psychotherapy: Theory, Research and Practice, 84*(3), 239–255. doi:10.1348/147608310X526511.

Gilbert, P., McEwan, K., Catarino, F., Baião, R., & Palmeira, L. (2014). Fears of happiness and compassion in relationship with depression, alexithymia, and attachment security in a depressed sample. *British Journal of Clinical Psychology, 53,* 228–244. doi: 10.1111/bjc.12037.

Gilbert, P, Miles, J. (Eds.) (2002). *Body shame: Conceptualisation, research and treatment.* Suffolk, UK: Routledge.

Hanh, T. N. (1999). *Walking meditation. Call me by my true names: The collected poems of Thich Nhat Hanh* (p. 194). Berkeley, CA: Parallax Press

Hanh, T. N. (1975). *The Miracle of Mindfulness.* Boston, MA: Beacon Press.

Hanh. T.N. (1987). *Being Peace.* Berkeley, CA: Parallax Press

Herman, J. L. (1992). *Trauma and recovery.* New York: Basic Books.

Junger, S. (2016). Tribe: On Homecoming and Belonging. New York: Twelve/Grand Central Publishing.

Katherine, A. (1993). *Boundaries: Where you end and I begin.* NY: Fireside/Simon & Shuster.

Klein, J. (1989). *I Am.* Salisbury, UK: Non-Duality Press, Third Millennium Publications.

Kornfield, J. (1993). *A Path with Heart.* London, UK: Bantam Press.

Kṛpālvānanda, S. (1977). *Science of meditation.* Kayavarohan, Gujarat, India: Shri Dahyabhai Hirabhai Patel.

Lanius, U., Paulsen, S., & Corrigan, F. (2014). *Neurobiology and treatment of traumatic dissociation: Toward an embodied self.* New York, New York: Springer Publishing.

Levine, P. (1997). *Waking the tiger: Healing trauma.* Berkeley, CA: North Atlantic Books.

McDonald, K. (2005). *How to Meditate: A Practical Guide.* Somerville, MA: Wisdom Publications.

Muktananda. (1992). *I am that: The science of hamsa from the Vijñāna Bhairava.* South Fallsburg, NY: SYDA Foundation.

Muni, R. (1994). *Awakening life force: The philosophy and psychology of "spontaneous yoga.* St. Paul, MN: Llewelyn Press.

Napier, N. (1994). *Getting Through the Day. Strategies for Adults Hurt as Children.* New York, NY: W. W. Norton & Company.

Napier, N. (1996). *Recreating Your Self: Building Self-Esteem Through Imagining and Self-Hypnosis.* New York, NY: W. W. Norton & Company.

Neff, Kristin. (2011). *Self-compassion: Stop beating yourself up and leave insecurity behind.* New York: HarperCollins.

O'Donohue, J. (1999). *Eternal Echoes: Celtic Reflections on Our Yearning to Belong.* New York, NY: Harper Collins.

Ogden, P. (2006). *Trauma and the Body.* New York, NY: W. W. Norton & Company.

Oliver, M. (1986). *The Journey, Dream Work.* New York, NY: Atlantic Monthly Press.

Pema Chödrön. (1994). *Start Where You Are: A Guide to Compassionate Living.* Boulder, CO: Shambhala Publications.

Pema Chödrön. (1997). *When Things Fall Apart.* Boulder, CO: Shambhala Publications.

Rothschild, B. (2000.) *The Body Remembers.* New York, NY: W. W. Norton & Company.

Salzberg, S. (1995). *Lovingkindness: The Revolutionary Art of Happiness.* Boulder, CO: Shambhala Publications.

Schwartz, R. (1995). *Internal Family Systems.* New York, NY: Guilford Press.

Van der Hart, O., Nijiuenhuis, E. & Steele, K. (2006). *The Haunted Self.* New York, NY: W. W. Norton & Company.

Van der Kolk, B. (1996). *Traumatic Stress: The Effects of Overwhelming Experience on Mind, Body, and Society.* New York, NY: Guilford Press.

Weintraub, A. (2004). *Yoga for Depression: A Compassionate Guide to Relieve Suffering Through Yoga.* New York, NY: Broadway Books.

White, M. (2007). *Maps of Narrative Therapy. 2007.* New York, NY: W.W. Norton & Company.

Whyte, D. (1996). *The House of Belonging.* Langley, WA: Many Rivers Press

ABOUT THE AUTHOR

Deirdre Fay, MSW has decades of experience exploring the intersection of trauma, attachment, yoga and meditation, and teaches "a radically positive approach to healing trauma." Deirdre founded the Becoming Safely Embodied skills, the basis for this book, a manual of the same name, and is the author of *Attachment-Based Yoga & Meditation for Trauma Recovery* and co-author of *Attachment Disturbances for Adults,* as well as the co-author of chapters in *Neurobiological Treatments of Traumatic Dissociation.*

A former supervisor at The Trauma Center, Sensorimotor Psychotherapy Institute trainer from 2000–2008, Deirdre integrates contemporary models of healing, including Compassion Focused Therapy, Internal Family Therapy, and her experience as a qualified trainer in Mindful Self-Compassion, and former board member of the New England Society for the Study of Trauma and Dissociation. Additionally, Deirdre is trained in Self-Awakening Yoga and LifeForce Yoga. She is a respected international teacher and mentor for working safely with the body. She recently leapt across the pond and is now residing with her husband in the South of France.

www.ingramcontent.com/pod-product-compliance
Lightning Source LLC
Jackson TN
JSHW080857211224
75817JS00003B/99